FINDING A
FAITH
THAT MAKES
SENSE

D1166564

FINDING A
FAITH
THAT MAKES
SENSE

By
R. SCOTT COLGLAZIER

Chalice Press
St. Louis, Missouri

Cover design and art: Bob Watkins
Art Director: Michael Domínguez

10 9 8 7 6 5 4 3 2   97 98 99 00

Library of Congress Cataloging-in-Publication Data

Colglazier, R. Scott, 1956-
    Finding a faith that makes sense / R. Scott Colglazier.
        p.   cm.
    Includes bibliographical references.
    ISBN 0-8272-1020-5
    1. Theology, Doctrinal—Popular works.   I. Title.
BT77.C685   1996
230—dc20
                                                      96-14008
                                                          CIP

Printed in the United States of America

CONTENTS

ACKNOWLEDGMENTS

I need to thank so many people who have helped me in the process of my own theological growth. Some of that assistance has come from professional theologians and scholars such as Clark Williamson and Ronald Allen of Christian Theological Seminary, and Michael Kinnamon, now of Lexington Theological Seminary. Do not hold any of them accountable for what is written in this book. I have developed in different directions since those student days, but there is no denying that they got me started in my theological process and for that I am grateful.

I owe a great deal to Brother David Steindl-Rast, who has been my friend and teacher over the last decade. Although a monk and mystic, he always seemed to make time for my visits to California, and I cherish our times together. Our conversations at the New Camaldolese Monastery in Big Sur, California, and at the Esalen Institute have changed my life.

My colleagues in ministry, such as Jerry and Diane Zehr, have taught me the meaning of my life over and over again in countless conversations. Don Jones has been one of the best friends I've ever had and has taught me much about the sheer gift of being human. My present colleague, Kathy Palen, provided valuable assistance with the final reading of this manuscript. I also must remember friends like Dale Martlage and his wife, Cheryl. For the last ten years, Dale has been one of the most important conversation partners in my life and always has time for me when I need a friend or a place to stay in California.

Then there are my congregations—people and places where my ideas have floated and sunk, soared and crashed. The privilege of teaching and learning from these people has been immeasurable. Many thanks to the folks at Southport Christian Church (Disciples of Christ) of Indianapolis, Indiana, and my current place of ministry, Beargrass Christian Church (Disciples of Christ) in Louisville, Kentucky. At both of these places I have made lifelong friends who have been interested in my thinking and writing. Listening to the people in these places has shaped this project probably more than I will ever know. Neither of these churches always agreed with me, but we knew how to be a church together as we became companions in the adventure of learning. I'm also grateful for my administrative assistant, Karen Mann, who reads everything I write with her helpful editor's eye.

Finally, I must mention my children: Matthew, Drew, and Katie. They continued being patient when they asked time and time again, "Is Dad still writing?" They are wonderful kids. The addition of our black Labrador, Lucy, has convinced me that sometimes angels come in the form of dogs! We wrote a lot of chapters together. And to Marti, my first love, my only wife, and my life companion—you have read every word I've ever written, and you are written in every word. To you this work is dedicated.

INTRODUCTION

Why does thinking theologically matter? In some ways that's like asking, "Why does my life matter?" or "Why does it matter how we live in the world?" or "Why is it important that we discover meaning in life?" It just does!

In some ways it's impossible not to think theologically. If you think about what your life means to you or if you've ever stopped and reflected on what life is all about, then you have already started the work of a theologian. Having been a parish minister for several years now, I'm convinced that people are thinking theologically all the time. Folks may not be aware that they're thinking theologically, but they are. Any question about what life ultimately means is, in the end, a theological question.

However—and this is why I offer this book to you—I believe that some ways of thinking are better than others, that certain ways of understanding God make more sense than other ways, and that certain perspectives of the Christian faith need to be heard, even if they were not learned in Sunday school as a child.

It is not that I have all the answers or that I think my way of thinking is better than everyone else's. I don't. I continue to learn and grow and change. I am indebted to the many people in my church who join me each week in trying to understand the good news of God better and to experience God more fully. I think, finally, that what matters most in our relationship with God is not how we explain the faith, but how we experience it.

1

At the same time, many ways of thinking about the Christian faith don't make sense to me as they are presented by some people. This does not mean that certain people or churches are not sincere. I'm sure they are. It simply means that it is important to have a faith that "adds up," a faith that is coherent and makes sense, a faith that doesn't ask people to check their brain in the foyer before they walk into the church. Finding a faith that makes sense has been for me a lifetime quest. I want mystery and enchantment, to be sure. However, mystery should never be confused with nonsense, and confusion should never be presented in the place of genuine enchantment with God.

There is a variety of authentic Christian voices across the broad spectrum of the church. There is not one Christian voice, but several. I try to offer one kind of Christian voice in this book. It is not the only Christian voice, but it's one that is at least worth considering. You who have come from a more conservative Christian background will probably recognize that I'm presenting the Christian faith in a way that is different from what you are used to. I want to encourage you to be patient with some of these new perspectives. I've always believed that one of the fundamental gestures of faith is to have an open mind and be about the business of growing and changing. Your faith, as well as my own, can grow and deepen.

One of the most alarming features of the so-called "Christian Right" in this country is that it seems to present a faith that leaves no room for discussion or honest differences of perspective. In this book, I try to offer a view of the Christian faith that is balanced, coherent, and sensible. More important, I try to give a picture of the faith that is open, tolerant, interesting, connected to real life, and passionately truthful. What I know to be true is that all that I write is offered in the spirit of love and adventure.

I need to alert you to what this book is and is not. This is not an academic work. I hope it is intellectually authentic, but it is not in the least a scholarly work nor is it written for clergy colleagues. I've tried to write a book that is simple without being simplistic. This has proven to be more of a challenge than I had ever imagined. This book is written for those who sit in the pews Sunday after Sunday, for people who would like to learn a little more, think about their faith a little more clearly, and get started in the journey of Christian growth. This is the kind of book a pastor would want to put in the hands of a layperson and say, "Here, read this." "Use this in your Sunday school class." "I think you might enjoy this." "Read it, and let's get together and talk about it over lunch." If the book can be shared in this way, I will have succeeded in my original intention.

I've designed each chapter to be about a "sermon and a half" in length, thus making the book time-accessible for people who are living in a busy world. In some ways I see this as a beginner's book. I don't use the word *beginner* in a condescending way. I simply mean that this book is for those who want to take a look at some basic Christian ideas and to use it as a beginning point.

The format of the book is relatively simple and straightforward. It has four sections with three chapters in each section. Each chapter begins with a reflection text and ends with a series of discussion questions. In addition to an individual reading, an adult church school class or a study group might use this book over a period of several weeks. I use the Bible extensively because, from my experience in congregations, I believe people are hungering to learn more about the Bible. Obviously the Bible is a great resource for deepening our spiritual lives. Throughout each chapter I use stories and experiences to help break open the ideas I want to convey. Throughout the book I have tried to be authentic with my own experiences of life and honest about sharing those experiences with you. Even as I have tried to listen to my life, I would encourage you to discover the gift of listening to your own life, to explore your feelings and ideas and experiences, and to let listening become a spiritual key in your quest of God.

The first section is on the Bible. The three chapters in this section are all designed, in one way or another, to help people understand what the Bible is and what the Bible is not. Too many people want the Bible to be something it is not. This is unfair to the Bible, as well as to ourselves. The Bible can make a tremendous difference in our lives, but the Bible should be understood for what it is and not forced to be something it was never intended to be. In fact, some of these interpretations and approaches to the Bible can create deep spiritual damage. I do not, for example, take a literalistic, legalistic, or mechanistic approach to the Bible. The Bible evolved through many centuries in the life of Israel and the church and should be appreciated, not only for what it says, but also for why it says what it says.

In the second section I address the experience of prayer. To talk about prayer is to talk about how God works in the world and how we live a spiritual life. To say this section is about prayer is really a way of saying it is about God. We always pray our theology. This section is the most explicitly theological section of the book and raises the deepest questions people have about how God works in this world. There is tremendous interest today in spirituality. Personally, I'm thrilled to see this renewed interest in questions of soulfulness and ultimacy. I know that the driving force in my life over the last decade has become the development of my spirituality. Spirituality has become more broadly defined today than I had ever imagined it in years past and for that I'm grateful. Whether you are talking about prayer or meditation or spiritual direction or dream analysis or vision quests or retreats at monastic retreat centers, you are talking about prayer. Thomas Merton in his writings and David Steindl-Rast in his friendship with me have helped me understand that all of life is prayer. But prayer is always theological.

In the third section I address the topic of Jesus. Where do you start to talk about Jesus? There are so many facets to his life and so many legitimate approaches to understanding his life. Literally centuries of theological ideas have been built around his life. In this section I had especially to keep in mind that this is a book of beginnings, and that there was no way I could give the figure of Jesus a comprehensive treatment. Therefore, I chose to talk about the formation of the Gospels, since for most people who attend church these are the primary writings we use to learn about Jesus. I try to help people understand how we know what we know about Jesus through these Gospel documents called Matthew, Mark, Luke, and John. Following that, I turn my attention to the meaning of his death on the cross and his resurrection. I'm sure some will criticize and say, "Why didn't he talk about such and such...?" I understand the criticism. At the same time, I think these three chapters on Jesus are, at a minimum, a good beginning place. I present in these chapters an alternative way of understanding Jesus, one probably different from what is commonly heard from more traditional presentations of the faith, but which has a certain degree of legitimacy.

In the fourth section I turn to the presence and experience of the Holy Spirit. When people believe in Christ they receive the gift of God's very presence, the Holy Spirit. What does the Spirit do for us? I address the possibilities of creativity, of hope, and of gifts of service to the world, all under the category of the Spirit. The Spirit is very important to me. Through the years I have become much more focused and aware of the Holy Spirit in my life and in the world. I'm afraid in years past I've underestimated the power of God's energy—spirit, breath, wind—in the world. No more. The Spirit moves life forward and empowers the church. I'm convinced that if there is to be hope for the ongoing renewal for the church it will happen through a renewal of mysticism and spirituality.

These four areas—Bible, Prayer, Jesus, Spirit—though not exhaustive of the Christian faith, become at least four corners in which the faith can be framed. As someone who enjoys photography, I have learned that often a photograph can dramatically jump to life if only the right frame is found. I hope these four areas can become a frame for you, bringing to life the very picture of God's good news for your life and for this world, a picture, though filled with mystery and wonder, that finally makes sense.

I

BIBLE

1

WHAT ABOUT THE
AUTHORITY
OF THE
BIBLE?

You desire truth in the inward being;
therefore teach me wisdom in my secret heart.
Purge me with hyssop, and I shall be clean;
wash me, and I shall be whiter than snow.
Let me hear joy and gladness;
let the bones that you have crushed rejoice.
Hide your face from my sins,
and blot out all my iniquities.

Create in me a clean heart, O God,
and put a new and right spirit within me.
Do not cast me away from your presence,
and do not take your holy spirit from me.
Restore to me the joy of your salvation,
and sustain in me a willing spirit.

Psalm 51:6–12

The Bible is the most controversial book in the world. It's not simply that people have different opinions about the Bible. They do, but it is also the case that people are deeply and emotionally divided over the Bible.

In most churches today, a subtle fault line runs through a congregation's membership over what the Bible is, how the Bible should be used, how the Bible should be interpreted, and how the Bible should be applied to daily life. Every minister knows too well that there is even disagreement over how the Bible should be preached from the pulpit.

You may be thinking, *"What's so controversial about the Bible?"* The truth is, virtually every controversial issue in the church is controversial because of the Bible. The issue really isn't—*Is the Bible authoritative for our lives?* The question most present in our churches is—*How is the Bible authoritative for our lives?* And that word—*how*—suggests the Bible is equipment for the church to utilize and employ for the well-being of a congregation. The Bible is a tool given to us by God and the faith community in order to keep faith alive and vibrant.

Frankly, I have become weary with the implications that the more fundamentalistic or conservative a church is the more its members follow the Bible, love the Bible, and take the Bible seriously. Often the implication is that these churches take the Bible much more seriously than members of mainline churches. I would encourage you to understand that just because a minister stands in the pulpit and rattles off Bible verse after Bible verse does not mean he is taking the Bible seriously or that the congregation necessarily is hearing a "biblical" sermon. Just because children go to Sunday school classes and learn to quote verses or can recite all the books of the Bible frontward and backward does not necessarily guarantee that the children have been encountered by a living word from God. I don't think that conservative, fundamentalistic churches take the Bible any more seriously or view it as any more authoritative than a typical Methodist or Presbyterian or Disciples congregation. The difference is *how* they use the Bible, *how* the Bible is understood, *how* the Bible is applied, and *how* the Bible is viewed as authoritative for Christians.

I believe Christians are supposed to utilize the Bible in a way that effectively develops faith. We need the Bible. The Bible can help inspire and direct the unfolding adventure of any Christian's life. I do think it is generally true that the more conservative churches have done a better job placing the Bible into the hands and hearts of their members in a way that is accessible and convenient. Every congregation without exception should be striving to do this.

Yet we don't come to church to worship the Bible and the Bible was never intended to be the center focus of the church. The God we worship is bigger than the Bible. We can learn about Jesus Christ through the Bible, but Jesus Christ is always beyond the Bible. We worship God. We follow Jesus Christ. The Bible can help us in our faith, and if used properly, it enhances our worship and quest of discipleship.

If you are a woodworker or an auto mechanic, you know a piece of equipment is useless if it is used improperly. In fact, a piece of equipment is downright dangerous if you don't use it properly. A piece of equipment in the hands of a surgeon, for example, might save a life. In the hands of a first-year medical student, however, it might become an instrument of tragedy. Using a tool improperly might even be a little embarrassing.

I remember several years ago, when I was in college, I borrowed a friend's car to go on a date. My girlfriend and I went to a concert, and when we came out I saw that one of the tires was almost out of air. Well, you need to know that, both then and now, I know virtually nothing about cars (other than the fact that you needed one to go on a date). I didn't want to show my ignorance of not being able to change a tire in front of my girlfriend, so I decided there was enough air to get us to a gas station about a mile away. I started driving and luckily made it. I said to myself, "I'm home free!"

I got out of the car and said to her with my most authoritative male voice, "I'm going to take care of this flat tire." I felt so in control—the way a man wants to feel on a date with his girlfriend! She smiled at me. I smiled at her. I walked around to the flat tire and unscrewed the cap to the air nozzle. I gave her another little wave. She smiled and waved back at me. I pulled the hose close to the tire. No problem. Then, in front of my girlfriend's eyes, I pressed the handle . . . and out shot a blast of cold water! I mean lots of water! Now, in my defense, it was night. No doubt, it was a poorly lighted gas station. And the air hose was right next to the water hose. It really was! The equipment was just fine, but it was the operator of the equipment who needed a little help.

Well, that might be a good way of thinking about the Bible. The Bible is a great piece of equipment for our Christian journey, but a few basic guidelines on how to use that equipment might save us a lot of grief and even some embarrassment.

It's interesting to me that often in the ministry of Jesus huge controversies would boil up over his way of using the Bible. For instance, some folks around Jesus would use the Bible to contend that certain kinds of behavior were acceptable or unacceptable on the Sabbath. Jesus, on the other hand, would suggest other kinds of behavior were acceptable or unacceptable as part of the Sabbath day observance. What's amazing is that *both* sides were using the Bible! Yet, for Jesus, the Bible was not a book to quote at people like a tossed hand grenade, nor was it a book to yell from in order to shout down those who differed from him. Unfortunately, many today feel justified in using the Bible exactly this way. Jesus reasoned with people from the Bible. He used the Bible in a way that enhanced the religious life of his followers. In fact, one of the best dynamic traditions from Israel is how Jewish scholars would utilize the Bible in a creative and ongoing way. Jesus himself used the Bible as a piece of equipment, a vital resource to help people discover a deeper sense of God in their lives.

I want to offer you three guidelines for effectively using the Bible. Actually these guidelines could help you as you study for a Sunday school class or listen to a sermon in church or even provide a little assistance when you listen to anyone talk about the Christian faith. These guidelines might even help you discern articles you read in the newspaper about religious issues or help you sort out what seems to be endless controversies about our faith in both church and society. The guidelines are in the form of questions that I think you should utilize every time you read the Bible.

The first guiding question to using the Bible is: *Does this passage from the Bible make sense?* By this question, I don't mean to imply, "Do you understand every single detail in the text?" Instead, I'm suggesting that you ask a question of sensibility. Does this text make sense in light of what you understand to be true about reality at the beginning of the twenty-first century? Is this text coherent in the world of reality that is generally accepted as true? It's important to remember that the Bible was written thousands of years ago. It is profoundly an ancient book! What was once true or thought to be true or accepted as true has changed dramatically through the years. There is new knowledge. There is new information. New facts emerge every day. We can't pretend when we read the Bible that these advances of knowledge have not taken place. That would be like an ostrich hiding its head in the sand. Therefore every time we read the Bible, we need to ask, *"Does this passage make sense?"*

What if I told you that last week I got a call from the local sheriff? The sheriff said to me: "Reverend, there is one of your church members talking nonstop over at Cave Hill Cemetery. He is yelling and screaming and jabbering senselessly. Why, he is even taking stones and hitting his own body, and it's bleeding and bruised. When we asked him whom we could call, he gave us your number! Reverend, what do you think we should do?"

Now, if I believe the Bible is to be authoritative in a literalistic way, I would have to say to the sheriff: "Officer, I'm sorry for the inconvenience but, you see, this is what has happened. Flying through the air are these little invisible creatures we call demons. Demons live in the middle of the earth where it is hot and flames never go out. Anyway, what happens is, the Devil lets some of these demons out into the atmosphere, and it sounds to me like one of the demons has flown into the body of one of my parishioners. It happens sometimes. In fact, you never can tell when it'll happen. I'll go over to my office and begin praying for him, and he should be better in a few minutes."

Do you see that's *one* way of using the equipment of the Bible? It is using the idea of demon possession, a common way of understanding reality in the first-century world and expressed frequently in the Bible, and applying that understanding of reality literally to our situation today.

A completely different response to this officer might have been: "Officer, I do know this man. I know he has a history of psychological problems. He's battled schizophrenia and depression for many years now. Or maybe he's having a reaction to medication. Or maybe he's had some kind of head injury causing him to act this way. Did you check the man for injuries? Or maybe he's using drugs, and he's having a bad trip. Or maybe he's heard some traumatic news and is having a strong emotional reaction. I'll call his doctor, and we'll make sure he gets some help. I'll call his family too. They will be very supportive. And I will pray for him too, because what we want for him more than anything is to be restored to wholeness. I want him to know that God will use all of these methods to achieve the restoration of his health. Officer, thanks for all your help."

Now, which approach makes the most sense? Both approaches use the Bible. Both approaches are deeply religious. Both approaches are used by churches.

Let me ask the question a little differently. If this person were one of your family members, perhaps your son or daughter, which approach would be most helpful to you? Which approach would most make the presence of God known to this hurting person? If this hurting person were your child, which approach would you most appreciate?

Just because something is said in the Bible at a literal level does not mean that it applies to our world today or that the Bible's view of reality is to be accepted for all time. We now know invisible flying creatures do not live in the atmosphere. There are other more sensible explanations for the bizarre behavior that I have just described. We now know that in the middle of the earth there is not a room with a red devil holding a pitchfork, sporting a tail, and just waiting to release his canary-like demons into the air. We know that particular version of reality is not a sensible or credible way of understanding life. That may have been part of an ancient cosmology (a way of looking at the universe), but it is not a cosmology that makes sense today. Geologists, just to name one particular discipline, have taught us that the middle of the earth is nothing but hot molten rock and certainly, not probably but certainly, no sustainable life is there.

The Bible is authoritative for the church today, but that is not the same as saying that ancient cultures and ancient viewpoints and ancient perceptions and ancient cosmologies are authoritative. The Bible envisioned an earth that had four corners and was a square, but we now know that such a geographical viewpoint was mistaken. We have traveled into space. We sat on the moon, turned around, and took pictures. The earth is round! The earth is not square regardless of what it says in the Bible. Therefore, to use the Bible with some degree of accuracy, much like an important piece of equipment, the question we must always ask is—*Does this passage from the Bible make sense?*

The second guiding question that I think is important for understanding the Bible in a credible way for our lives today is—*Is this Bible passage moral?* By moral, I mean, does this particular passage of the Bible contribute to the dignity of all God's creation? That's the essence of morality. Every time we hear the Bible being read or we hear a sermon based on the Bible or we hear people standing around the water fountain discussing religious topics in our office, it is crucial to ask this question. Just because it comes from a minister or is said in a church or is associated with the Bible does not mean that it represents this highest moral vision, a vision that calls for the dignity of all God's children in the world.

Jesus portrayed a remarkable vision of morality with persons throughout his ministry. When one group vehemently accused him, saying, "You have transgressed the Bible by healing a man on the Sabbath, which is work on the Sabbath and which is prohibited by the Bible; therefore, you did a religious no-no," Jesus did not respond by saying, "Well, the Bible does say that we should observe the Sabbath. I'm sorry. I guess I'm wrong."

Jesus knew that just because someone quoted the Bible didn't automatically mean that person had the Bible's deepest meaning at heart. Instead, like a skillful Jewish interpreter of the scripture, Jesus responded with deep human empathy by moving into the deepest moral wisdom of the Bible. "Look," he said, "isn't it *moral* to heal someone, to restore a person to wholeness? Isn't it *moral* to help someone find her life again and assist her in becoming the person God created her to be? Isn't it *moral* to do something profoundly good on the Sabbath? If you lost a sheep on the Sabbath wouldn't it be *morally* superior to help it out of the ditch rather than letting it lie there and die? And if it were always immoral to work on the Sabbath, then the minister could never conduct the Sabbath services because conducting a service is certainly work!" When his few critics heard this kind of deep moral wisdom, they walked away stunned. And well they should be, as should everyone who tries to use the Bible in a literalistic, narrow, and legalistic way.

Every Bible passage that is read needs to address the question of moral quality. Not every passage in the Bible is consistent with the deep moral wisdom present in the life of Jesus. I can show you, for example, places in the Bible where masses of people, including children, were killed in the name of God. Is that a kind of morality that is part of the Christian faith? I can show you places in the Bible that portray a kind of philosophy whereby people who are sick should not be touched and should not be allowed to be part of the worshiping community because they are considered unclean. Is that the kind of morality portrayed by Jesus? Is that the highest degree of morality associated with the good news of Jesus Christ, which is God's message of love toward all persons? I can show you places in the Bible where, if a couple couldn't have a baby, the wife was sent away in shame and a pinch hitter of a woman was brought into the picture for the sole reason of childbearing. Is that practice morally appropriate to the dignity of all God's children? Is that our view of morality regarding women and relationships? There are passages in the Bible that blatantly portray a pernicious anti-Jewish bias. Is such a bias acceptable within the deepest framework of the church?

I mention these examples simply to make the point that everyone who uses the Bible must recognize that not everything in the Bible is morally appropriate for Christians in the world today. Each generation is part of a moral evolution; each generation must wrestle with the deepest indignities of God's creation; and each generation must discover the deepest moral wisdom needed for its time. Sometimes the Bible will help us directly with moral matters; sometimes the Bible will help us indirectly with moral issues by suggestion and hints of moral direction; and sometimes the Bible will need to be understood clearly and then resisted because the passage is suggesting a morality that runs counter to the spirit of Jesus Christ. Regardless, the reader of the Bible has the opportunity to discover the deepest moral wisdom that runs throughout the Bible, and the ongoing discovery of that wisdom is what should be authoritative in guiding the life of the church.

The third guiding question I offer is—*Is this Bible passage consistent with the good news message of Jesus Christ?* I want you to know that it doesn't matter if the passage is from the Old Testament or New Testament, or whether it is a passage that comes from one of my sermons or the sermon of a television evangelist, famous or infamous. It doesn't matter if the Bible passage is the centerpiece of a Sunday school class long cherished in a church. When reading the Bible, the question that always emerges is—*Is this Bible passage consistent with the good news message of Jesus Christ?*

Now, there are a variety of legitimate ways of talking about the gospel, but one way that continues to make sense to me is— *The gospel is God's good news of unconditional love extended to all creation and God's call to be fully alive to that gift of love in the spirit of community.*

Certainly a love energy radiated from the life of Jesus. Jesus radically lived the gospel when he ate with religious and social outcasts. He went home with Zacchaeus, the outcast tax collector, and that signaled to Zacchaeus that indeed God would come home with him. This was remarkably good news for a man who had come to believe that God would never be allowed to come home to his life. In Jesus' stories about the prodigal son and the wedding feast attended by the poor, Jesus was revealing a God who was ready to love the unlovable and to call back to life those whose lives had gone dead. Imagine that! Even the spiritually dead were loved and brought back to life! Whether it was feeding the hungry crowds or touching the suffering leper or holding a cast-off orphan in his arms, Jesus was present with people, and his presence revealed the energy of God's love.

Tom Peters, in his recent book *The Pursuit of Wow!*, writes of how people and corporations make decisions about operating with a wonderful quality he calls, "Wow!" Wow is the experience of someone's going the extra mile, doing the unexpected, revealing creativity, unleashing energy that brings healing, making a difference in people's lives. That's wow! Wow is wonderful!

Jesus too lived with wow! His wow revealed a good-news God, not a bad-news God. His wow revealed a God ready to love, not ready to push away. His wow revealed a God who picks people up after they make mistakes, not pushes people's noses down even further in those mistakes. The God of Jesus is a wow God of acceptance, not a woe God of fear. That's the wow of the essence of the good news. Even the cruelty of a Roman cross couldn't stop the Jesus-Wow from filling the world. He wowed them even more by coming back to life through his resurrection, living through his disciples, and living even today as we feel his presence in our lives.

It continues to be clear to me that people make decisions to think of God in one of three ways. We think of God as a punishing God, ready to zap us when we do something wrong and step out of line. Or we think of God as an indifferent God, not genuinely related or interested in the well-being of the world. Or we think of God as a loving God, ready to embrace us, heal us, and call us into the deepest experience of life. Part of the Wow! of Jesus was that he announced a God whose very definition was unconditional love and grace.

I loved the movie *City Slickers*. It's the story of three middle-aged men who go to a dude ranch for a couple of weeks to learn how to be cowboys. Each of them is in his own life crisis, and each of them, in his own personal way, is searching for some missing piece of his life. One character, named Phil, is in pain over a broken marriage and the end of his career. One night around the campfire he breaks down in tears. He sobs and contemplates taking his own life. He senses the hopelessness of his situation. Yet, his two best buddies hold him, comfort him, and talk to him. Finally, one of them captures just the right sentiment when he says, "Phil, don't you see that you have a 'do-over'? Just like when we were kids playing baseball, you have a 'do-over.'"

In many ways the good news message of God is that God gives us a "do-over." Not just every now and then, but daily, sometimes hourly, God gives us a "do-over." That's what the reflection text, Psalm 51, was about at the beginning of this chapter. God creates the heart all over again. God restores spirit, breath, life into our lifeless bodies. God lets us feel joy again. A "do-over!" That's the good news.

When any Bible passage is read, the reader should ask, *What is the good news in this passage?* Because that is finally what we all are seeking. We read the Bible for the good news experience. A hymn, which sometimes is used in church, says, "Beyond the sacred page, I seek thee Lord; My spirit pants for thee, O living Word." That's the living, breathing, transforming stuff of the Bible. Sure, there are lots of words in the Bible, even lots of interesting information in the Bible. But there is finally one word that we seek in the midst of all the Bible's words, and that is the word, the personal dialogue with the very presence of God. This is why "revelation" is always more than the mere presentation of the Bible; religious revelation is an encounter with our lives and the life of God. That's where truth is found; it's where the good news is found.

Does the Bible apply to our lives? That depends on how you use it. If you try to apply every literal word to our lives today, then you have nothing left but a crazy impossibility or a maze of endless contradictions and inconsistencies. But if you try to follow these guiding questions—*Does the passage make sense? Is the passage moral? Does the passage fit with the gospel?*—then the Bible jumps with energy and relevance because it helps us find what the Christian faith is all about—discovering anew ourselves, our neighbor, and our God. That's always the goal of reading the Bible.

I don't want to exaggerate the importance of using the Bible in a way that makes sense, but there is episode after episode of people's using the Bible in a way that is tragic. The most recent one highlighted in our national consciousness was the use of the Bible by David Koresh and the Branch Davidian group in Waco, Texas. What was that tragedy all about? Why the senseless loss of life, especially the lives of children and brave government officials? Why the burning inferno and the mind-boggling tragedy? It would not be too simplistic to say that what happened in Waco, Texas, happened because one man and his followers tried to use the Bible in a literalistic, unreasonable, and uninformed way. Their biblical literalism of the book of Revelation set them up to believe they were God's last righteous people on this earth. In all likelihood they believed this persecution and even the exploding inferno were predicted in the Bible.

Extreme? Of course it's extreme, but the root problem begins with the failure to interpret the Bible in a way *that makes sense, that is moral, and that is consistent with the good news of God's love.* In the state of Kentucky, a man recently was killed at a church service. Why? Because he was handling a poisonous rattlesnake, and in so doing he was trying to follow the literalistic commands of the Bible. Yet that literal and unbalanced approach to the Bible finally became tragic. The exclusion of women from the leadership of the church is a tragic example of biblical literalism. The rise of so-called faith healers who rob millions of dollars from people is a tragic misuse of the Bible. The sentiment of hatred against Jews sometimes has been rooted in a literalistic interpretation of the Bible. I could cite many other examples, but the truth is—if the Bible is not understood in a way that makes sense, then the Bible becomes either irrelevant or irreversibly dangerous.

The church needs the Bible. I need the Bible in my life. The words and stories of Scripture nurture my life. And if you are trying to grow in your faith, you need the Bible too. Is the Bible easy to understand? Not always. Does everything in the Bible apply to our lives today? Not necessarily. Is it worth it, however, to read and study and explore the Bible? The answer is a resoundingly clear yes! When the Bible is used in a responsible and coherent way, it can transform our ideas, become food for our soul, and, most importantly, open the door for the living presence of God to touch our lives.

QUESTIONS FOR REFLECTION AND DISCUSSION

1. Discuss any real-life situations in which the Bible was used by people in a damaging way.
2. Why is it important that the Bible make sense?
3. What do you think is the highest moral vision to which Christians are called to live?
4. What would you say if someone off the street were to ask you, "What is your definition of the gospel?"
5. Can you recall a time when you read the Bible, enjoyed it, and really got something out of it? What made the positive difference in that experience of study?

2

Is There a
DIFFERENCE
Between the Word of God
AND THE BIBLE?

But a man named Ananias, with the consent of his wife Sapphira, sold a piece of property; with his wife's knowledge, he kept back some of the proceeds, and brought only a part and laid it at the apostles' feet. "Ananias," Peter asked, "why has Satan filled your heart to lie to the Holy Spirit and to keep back part of the proceeds of the land? While it remained unsold, did it not remain your own? And after it was sold, were not the proceeds at your disposal? How is it that you have contrived this deed in your heart? You did not lie to us but to God!" Now when Ananias heard these words, he fell down and died. And great fear seized all who heard of it. The young men came and wrapped up his body, then carried him out and buried him.

After an interval of about three hours his wife came in, not knowing what had happened. Peter said to her, "Tell me whether you and your husband sold the land for such and such a price." And she said, "Yes, that was the price." Then Peter said to her, "How is it that you have agreed together to put the Spirit of the Lord to the test? Look, the feet of those who have buried your husband are at the door, and they will carry you out." Immediately she fell down at his feet and died. When the young men came in they found her dead, so they carried her out and buried her beside her husband. And great fear seized the whole church and all who heard of these things.

Acts 5:1–11

This is one of those strange texts found in the Bible that frankly discourages people from reading the Bible. It is peculiar. It is, in one sense, reprehensible if this text is portraying a God who kills people because they don't give enough money to the church. It represents a peculiar picture of the church, a church of a different time and place and culture. This is neither the church nor the context where most of us find ourselves each week on Sunday morning. It is one of those peculiar texts that reminds us that there is a significant distance between our lives today and the ancient world of the Bible. And frankly, keeping that distance in mind is a helpful insight when trying to read the Bible for our day and our situation. Interestingly enough, the peculiar nature of this Bible reading makes it a good example of how to read the Bible in a more effective way. The question this text raises is simple—*Is there a difference between the word of God and the Bible?*

Frequently people come up to me and say, "At our church we just preach the Bible. We follow the Bible literally. If it is in the Bible, then that is the word of God. We believe in the complete inerrancy of the Bible." Sometimes people ask me, "Do you believe that the Bible is the inspired word of God, inerrant, and one-hundred percent infallible?"

I understand that when people talk about the Bible in this way they are trying to recognize the Bible as important and essential to the Christian life. And I deeply appreciate the fact that people and churches would take time to use the Bible, read the Bible, and submit their lives to the teachings of the Bible. At the same time, I think all questions that in one way or another attempt to equate the word of God with the literal words written in the Bible are misguided and, strangely enough, hurt the Christian faith as opposed to helping it.

When I stand in the pulpit of my congregation, I don't think it's my job to preach the Bible. I certainly want to use the Bible in the pulpit. And I do. I could use the Bible in various ways to reach the hearts of members of my church. And I do that as well. But the job of the church and those who fill the pulpits has never been to preach the Bible. After all, the church community existed for years without a Bible from which it could preach! For years the early church had no written account of the life of Jesus. Nevertheless, its members preached the word of God every Sunday. The Jewish community you read about in the Hebrew Scriptures existed for years without a written Bible. They told and retold, interpreted and reinterpreted the stories of their faith; but the actual written words came much later in their history, and even those writings were many times compilations of stories that came from different times and places in the expansive life of the Jews. Obviously there is something bigger to be preached and something bigger to be heard than merely written words on the page.

I like to think of it this way: there is the Bible, the words and sentences of the Bible, the stories of the Bible, the many tales and insights of the Bible. And then there is the word of God. By word of God, I mean big "W" Word! This is the living Word, the creative Word, the Word that is in its essence the divine reality, the Word that animates the entire universe. This is the Word that is the presence of God, everlasting, personal, and a Word that invites from us participation, dialogue, and engagement. And that's exactly what I try to preach every time I step in the pulpit. It's what I'm after (and what also is after me!) every time I read the Bible. Every time I go to Sunday school. Every time I listen to a sermon. Every time I lead a Bible study. What is trying to break through the words of the Bible is a living Word that can explode inside the human heart and make a transforming difference in the deepest part of my life. Indeed, the word of God is God's very presence.

When you read in the Gospel of John, "In the beginning was the Word, and the Word was with God, and the Word was God," John is not talking about pages and ink and sentences and paragraphs. John is after the big "W" Word! Therefore, the point of Bible study or sermons or Sunday school is not to repeat the Bible or quote the Bible like machine-gun fire in rapid succession. What is needed is nothing less than the discovery of the living relational word of God.

Early in the westward expansion of this country, miners traveled to California to find their fortune in gold. Anticipation of riches filled their hearts. Frequently they would do the back-breaking work of panning for gold. An unforgiving sun would beat down on their hollow bodies as they would bend over the flowing streams and shake their pans and strain the water and pick through the rock and sand in order to find that one gold nugget, that one glimmering piece of wealth that would change their lives forever.

In many ways, reading the Bible is like panning for gold. If every literal word of the Bible were to be applied directly to our contemporary lives, there would be a lot of rock and sand. Some of the Bible just doesn't pertain to us. Some of it just doesn't make sense for our time and culture. It's not that we shouldn't read and be familiar with those parts, it's just that they have little to do with contemporary faith experience.

But if we sift through the words of the Bible, the differences in culture, and the peculiarities of the Bible itself, we find the gold of God's good news and the gold of a transforming Word that makes a significant difference in our lives. I enjoy watching children read fairy tales because they instinctively understand that when there is gold in the story, gold becomes the most important pursuit of all. The same is true with the Bible. There is a difference between the words of the Bible and the living word of God, the gold we are after.

The reflection text from Acts is an exceptional example of the sifting process that is needed as we use the Bible. Looking at this text on the surface, we see an interesting if not disturbing plot. The early Christian community is portrayed as something of a commune. People were sharing equally in wealth. People were bringing their material possessions and throwing them into the common pot so all could have their economic needs met. Individuals didn't think so much in terms of "mine" as they thought in terms of "ours" or the "community." The common good was held to be more important than individual success. And the main impetus behind this organizational commune was to make sure people who were the most needy, such as widows and orphans, could

have all their economic needs met. Indeed, some people have tried
to suggest, using this Bible passage, that the early church practiced
a form of communism. I wouldn't go that far, but, without a doubt,
there are communal elements in this text.

Whether or not you or I like it, this particular way of being
church is in the Bible. That cannot be denied. Here it is! Yet in
spite of the distance and strangeness of this text, the church needs
to take this Bible passage seriously. Just because a Bible passage is
difficult does not mean that the passage can be ignored. In fact,
some of the most difficult passages found in the Bible need to be
heard by the church with extra clarity, because those passages offer
the richest potential for transformation.

It is the image of *listening and speaking* that I would suggest
must become central to the reading of any text of the Bible. We
need to *listen* to the text. Have you noticed that good listening
always requires genuine effort? How many times have we heard
the literal words of a friend or a spouse but missed the deeper,
underlying feelings of the conversation?

A few years ago my teenage son and I were talking about
some issue at home. I forget now what the issue was, but it was
one of those moments when he was unhappy with me and I was
unhappy with him and communication was getting worse by the
minute. Those of you who have kids probably have been there.
Finally, we called a truce, and he and I both walked away angry.
But when he was almost out of sight he yelled from the top of the
stairs, "We never talk about *topics* anymore!"

I thought, "That's a strange thing to say. Topics? What does
he mean by topics?" So we talked a little more. He shared with me
how he likes to sit out on our deck and just talk about different
topics, different subjects, ideas in which he is interested. I'm not
always the best at talking about homework and schedules for the
next day, but I do love the challenge of any theoretical discussion.
We talk about this movie or that movie. We talk about ideas. We
talk about books or television shows. That's one of the things we
do well as a family—sit out on the deck and talk together. However, we had gone through a busy time in our lives, and there had
been very few moments for those kinds of conversations. He and I
had been in a major conflict, and I thought it was over homework

or the messiness of his room or the fact that he hadn't mowed the lawn, but that really wasn't it. After listening, I mean really listening, I recognized what he was trying to say to me. He was trying but didn't know how to say, "I *miss* you! I want to spend time with you! I want to talk about something other than our busy family schedules!" What came home to me in that experience is that listening requires the deeper tuning in to the emotional message of a person. Relationships are 99 percent listening.

The Bible also invites that kind of listening. Merely to read and apply the surface words of a Bible passage is to miss the genuine feeling, the genuine insight, the applicable message that is living underneath the text and waiting to be set free to soar in the human heart like a beautiful hot-air balloon. Listening for the word of God that is found in the midst of the words of the Bible is an extraordinary act of faith. That also means that the point of reading the Bible is the enhancement of our relationship with God, not the mere gathering of surface facts of information from the Bible. A deep closeness with God can be discovered when the Bible is heard at a level of depth. And it's only at this level that the Bible is really experienced with enchantment and wonder.

However, we not only need to *listen* to the Bible, we also need to *speak* to the Bible. In this sense, the Bible is a conversation partner with us in life. I wish I had a record of the number of times I have heard wives say to me in my office during a counseling appointment, "I wish my husband would just talk with me." Or parents almost cry out in desperation, "Why won't our teenager talk with us?" This longing for conversation is a longing for relationship. There's no relationship without this genuine moment of conversation.

If the Bible is to help us discover a deeper relationship with God, then we not only need to listen to the claims God makes on us through the Bible, but we also need to speak our needs to the Bible. It is impossible, contrary to what some would like to suggest, to read the Bible in a vacuum. We cannot be totally objective while reading the Bible, nor should we be. We need to bring our world, our concerns, our spiritual needs, and our dreams and speak them to the Bible.

Today, as I worked on this chapter, I had a conversation with a mother in pain over her son's drunk driving charge. She felt so much disappointment in him. And at an even deeper level, she felt disappointment in herself. I talked to a woman who has been married twenty years, and her husband told her today he doesn't love her anymore. Think of that. "I don't love you anymore." Her self-esteem was lower than dust itself. I talked with a businessman who is trying to figure out how he can sell one property and buy a larger building for his growing business. He is facing significant economic challenge. I talked with a well-respected man in the community who is trying to find a new job after the age of fifty. He never dreamed he would be in this position, and he is feeling anger and embarrassment. I talked to my associate minister who is getting ready to move to another state because his wife has taken a new job, and he is uncertain what he will do or if he will find a church to serve.

Now, believe it or not, I had all of these conversations in the course of one day. One day! What I want to emphasize is that if these kinds of real-life conversations cannot be brought to the Bible, then the Bible is no use at all. The Bible invites these conversations. The Bible welcomes these real-life, everyday dilemmas. The Bible wants to be a net to catch all of our feelings. If you wait until you get it all together to begin reading the Bible, you will never read the Bible at all! The Bible is to be our life conversation partner even as God is our great listening friend. Therefore, if you are reading this book and have been thinking about starting to read the Bible, I encourage you to do it. But don't put your life on hold to read the Bible. Read the Bible in the midst of your life. Bring your questions. Bring your hurts. Bring your joys. Let this book become your conversation partner.

So what would it look like to have a conversation with a Bible passage as peculiar as the one found in Acts 5:1–11? In terms of listening, it might be helpful to make the distinction between the *what* of the text and the *how* of the text. The *what* is the effort of the early church to take care of those who were in need, especially widows and orphans. That's what was happening in that first-century context. Sometimes these needy folks were widows and orphans, but sometimes they were just people who were poor and needed help. What the early Christians were trying to achieve was a community of faith that took care of those who were in need; this was the essence of the ministry of the church.

This ministry, of course, was not invented by the early church. Those early Christians reached out toward those who were most needy because the one they confessed as Lord had done the same. They were trying to be faithful to the living Word that they had heard in the Jesus stories and that they shared with one another in the first church. Additionally, since the earliest Christians were also Jewish, they had practiced for generations the principle of caring for those in the world who were needy. This passage from the book of Acts is the story about how the "Jesus movement" continued on to become the "Jesus community." That's *what* was going on.

The *how* of this text was the method they utilized to accomplish the *what* of the ministry. And in this case, the method was a communal relationship that moved away from private ownership and toward the economic equalization of all people in the church community. The *how* was a particular first-century feature. The *what* is an indispensable element of a faithful church in all ages. *How* they did the ministry is different from *what* they were trying to do.

When the Bible is read in a sensitive way there are several *implications* for the life of Christians which can be discovered.

First of all, this text helps us see that all caring must be *grounded in daily reality and not spiritualized in the name of Christ*. Caring is not some romantic, spiritualized experience. Those of you who have cared for an elderly parent know how hard and demanding caring is. There is nothing spiritually pretty about caring for an AIDS patient or meeting the needs of an out-of-control adolescent. Caring is grounded in reality, and that reality is demanding. The fact that the early church would even attempt the communal care of one another in the name of Christ is to its credit and for our example as we try to be a present-day, caring community. Far too often the church romanticizes its caring. A program is started, and then a few months later it is abandoned. We quickly inflate a dream, only to see it punctured by the hard point of reality. Jesus said, "Don't build unless you first count the cost." This text reminds the church, and each of us individually, that in all our endeavors there is a cost.

This text is also a reminder that caring is an *economic relationship*. The fact is that caring is not just done with the heart; it is done with the billfold and pocketbook and checkbook. The economic implications of the gospel are not always easy to live out in our daily lives, but they are part of the calling God offers to each of us. At the end of Acts 4, there is the story of Barnabas, who sold a piece of land and brought all the proceeds and laid them at the apostles' feet. He did this out of his deep sense of mutual citizenship with other Christians. He did this because he felt the oneness of spirit and heart that existed in the church. That attitude of giving seems to be in stark contrast to much of the individualism and "what-will-I-get-out-of-this" attitude that many of us bring to our congregations. We glibly speak of church members today as "religious consumers." Unfortunately, the issue of common good is one of the great lost treasures of the church. Sure, we all want certain needs met in the church. I want to get something out of the church as much as the next person. At the same time, the first question, the primary question for Christians always has been— "What can I give to my church?" This is the vision of common good that is at the heart of the story in the reflection text.

This Bible story also makes a *claim about God.* The God presented in this story is both gift and demand, the one who comforts and disturbs. Indeed, God is a gift to us. God offers unconditional love to all persons and embraces us for who we are as people. God accepts our frailties and, at the same time, longs for us to actualize our potential. There were those in the early church who responded to the gracious God of good news by bringing gifts of joy and gratitude. The picture of their generosity is a picture of joyful response, not constraint, but wild and free response—as in the actions of Barnabas. This is the kind of joy and generosity that is appropriate to the gospel. Extravagant grace calls for nothing less than extravagant generosity.

This is why when we bring our offering to church each Sunday it is not merely paying our bill or making good on a reluctant commitment. On the contrary, if we have been "good newsed," if we have met the one who loves us unconditionally, then the only right response is to bring our gifts, to bring them often, and to bring them generously. I would suggest that you try something for one month. Try smiling the entire time of the offering. Smiling really can be a form of prayer and meditation. Smile from beginning to end! I guarantee that you will begin to feel more joy in the experience of giving.

This text, however, portrays a God who not only should have this response of joy, but who demands this response. Frequently we become uncomfortable with the concept of God's character demanding or asking something from us. One of my favorite *New Yorker* cartoons shows a minister in the pulpit ready to preach on the Ten Commandments. The caption has him backpedaling to his twentieth-century audience, saying, *"Now, this might sound a little authoritative . . . ."*

Could it be that many of us have grown *too* comfortable with God? Have we reduced God to nothing more than a cozy teddy bear? Being comfortable with God is wonderful, and we need that dimension as we live our lives. I think one of the worst ways of imagining and relating to God is to picture God as a punishing, menacing, "out-to-get-us" kind of being. But we cannot forget that God asks something of our lives—demands and expects a certain way of living from us. This is a kind of holy demand that calls forth our best, that calls forth a certain quality of discipleship, a certain quality of life that cannot be ignored or rationalized away.

I think of the various ways my mother and father related to me while I was growing up. I always knew they loved me. That was never in question. But often that love was expressed in the form of demands and expectations. They had certain expectations about homework, about how to behave at the dinner table, and about how I would conduct my life in public. I can still hear my mother yell up the stairs, "Scott, you forgot to take out the garbage!" And of course the real message was, "Get out of bed and get to work around here!" These kinds of expectations were expressed in the sentiment that a friend shared with me recently. She said, "Before I went out on a date, my mother would always say to me, 'Don't forget who you are!' And I still try to follow that wisdom." Not a bad expectation.

God's expectation for us to be generous givers is not the demand of a tyrant, but of a lover who wants loyalty and expressiveness in relationship. This is especially crucial for many of us who wrestle between spiritual values and the values of materialism. These two values, in reality, become competing gods between which we as Christians must choose. The god of materialism offers comfort and security and, to some degree, immortality. We look to wealth to do things for us. And it does. Money gives us power and comfort and security. However—and this is where we need to be clearminded in light of this biblical story—it is only a little power, a little comfort, and a little security.

A few years ago I was worshiping in a church that is probably one of the most affluent congregations in this country. But even in that church they still were saying prayers for members with cancer or heart disease or who were recovering from an automobile accident. Anne Morrow Lindbergh once wrote, "There is no aristocracy of grief. Grief is the great leveler." And it's true. Finally, money cannot be an ultimate value. To try to live every day in a relationship with God means that we seek our comfort, our security, and our immortality from the one who loves us and accepts us. Therefore, God not only calls us to this life as a gift to be received, God also expects us to live this life in a way that is fitting to the gift.

The other dimension of this text that I would suggest is beneath the literal surface is the *element of trust*. If you are a church member or active in any organization, you realize how important trust is. If trust is broken then the whole web of the organization vibrates with uncertainty. Once, one of my children lied to me, and it took time to rebuild trust. This is why when somebody says she will chair a committee at church, but she doesn't really deliver the goods of leadership, the entire structure of the church is broken. When a parent says he will be at a son's Little League game but doesn't show up, trust is broken. And when God gives the gift of unconditional love and there is not a lifestyle of generosity appropriate to that gift, then trust is broken. It's a powerful moment for a church when members learn how to trust one another and replace the suspicion and negativity that too often characterize congregations. The story of Ananias and Sapphira is a story of trust broken and community fractured.

What I want to suggest is that here is a story from the Bible that in its literal reading doesn't have much to say to the church. It speaks from a foreign time and place, offers a vision of God that is suspect, and presents a view of community that is virtually impossible to imitate today. I don't think the members of First Christian Church, Anywhere, or Christ Methodist, U.S.A., are ready to turn over their lives to become a commune!

In this text is a living, transforming, challenging word of God. It's a Word not found on the surface, but in the dynamic of the depth of the story itself. This Word is not the same as the literal words of the Bible. This Word requires a little theological reasoning and some plain old common sense. Folks in more conservative traditions who take the Bible literally and apply the Bible directly to their lives today, regardless of their sincerity, don't realize what they are doing. It is impossible to do, and it backfires by making the Bible more irrelevant than relevant. But if you can go below the surface of the text, there is a Word about community and discipleship and about what it means to live as a Christian that presents itself to the listener. Put the pan in the stream. Shake it! Sift it! Gold awaits!

I want to end by offering some questions you might use while reading the Bible. These questions are meant to be good theological questions that will help you move past the surface of the literal words in order to discover the life-changing, life-claiming Word of the good news that can be found in the Bible. These questions can be used every Sunday while you listen to the reading of the Bible or hear your minister's sermon. Bring these questions each week with you to your Sunday school class. Many times asking the right questions is more important than finding the right answers.

1. What is the larger, enduring message found in this reading from the Bible? This question helps sift through what is ancient historical context and what is applicable to our lives today. This question helps us find the gold of the underlying word that is found in the stories of the Bible.

2. To what is my soul drawn as I hear this Bible reading? People often ignore their own soulfulness while reading the Bible. I think it is fascinating to be aware of what you are drawn to in the Bible passage, what in the passage sparks your interest, what in the passage makes you say, "Aha, that's interesting!"

3. What is the vision of God presented in this Bible reading? This is a great question to ask of every reading and every sermon you hear. Bible stories paint portraits of God. What do you think of the portrait? Is there something in the portrait that you like or don't like? Is there something new here for you to consider?

4. What is the element of good news found in this Bible passage? It really doesn't matter if the passage is Old Testament or New Testament. Each passage we listen to is trying to speak some Word of good news, some golden message of meaning. Often when people read the Bible they get hung up like a fishing lure on a log over the details of the story. Always be looking for the fundamental good news message.

5. What is it in this Bible reading that belongs to another cultural time, and what is it that has the power to endure and change my life today? I want to say this as clearly as I can—The point of a Bible story is not to learn more about the Bible; it is to learn more about yourself as you walk before God. Not all of the Bible is relevant to our lives because it belongs to another culture and time. At the same time, underneath all the cultural and social trappings of the ancient world there is an enduring word that, when encountered, can change a person's life.

When people tell me, "We just follow the Bible and only the Bible in our church!"—I secretly want to say, "Oh, that's too bad. You should really try following Jesus Christ sometime." I don't say it, but I want to!

Yes, there *is* a difference between the good news, big "W" Word that is discovered through listening and speaking to the Bible and the literal words and sentences bound by culture and history that fill page after page of this book called the Bible. The literal words can lead us to the living presence of the Word, but only if we ask the questions that help us dive through the surface and face that which finally needs to be faced by all of us—God!

QUESTIONS FOR REFLECTION AND DISCUSSION

1. How would you fill in the blank? The Bible is
_____.
2. What's the difference between the Bible and the word of God?
3. Why is it so important to bring our real feelings and needs to the Bible?

4. If you were going to preach a sermon on this story of Ananias and Sapphira, what ideas would you try to communicate?
5. Using another familiar story from the Bible, try using the five questions presented at the end of the chapter and see what kind of answers you come up with.

3

HOW DO YOU
FIND
LIGHTS, CAMERA, AND
ACTION?

Then Jesus came from Galilee to John at the Jordan, to be baptized by him. John would have prevented him, saying, "I need to be baptized by you, and do you come to me?" But Jesus answered him, "Let it be so now; for it is proper for us in this way to fulfill all righteousness." Then he consented. And when Jesus had been baptized, just as he came up from the water, suddenly the heavens were opened to him and he saw the Spirit of God descending like a dove and alighting on him. And a voice from heaven said, "This is my Son, the Beloved, with whom I am well pleased."

Matthew 3:13–17

Everyone has a complex system of *religious authority*. You make religious decisions. You look at important matters in your life through the eyes of your faith. You reason about your religion. You have religious feelings that mean a great deal to you. You might not be able to explain exactly what your religious authority system is or how it works or even how you arrived at the point where you are today, but I guarantee there is some system inside your brain that sorts out how you think and how you feel and what you believe. You *cannot not* have a religious authority system.

I also want to suggest that not all religious authority systems are equal. That is to say, some religious authority systems just don't make sense; they make an unnecessary split between faith and reason. Some religious authority systems are downright oppressive. If you were brought up in a strict, legalistic style of religious faith, you probably understand that everything you do is done in order to avoid going to hell. Lots of shame. Lots of guilt. Very little life. That's a religious authority system. Some are utterly dangerous, even tragic in their implications and consequences. You can see this in cults that practically abduct the souls of young people and ruin their lives. But cults do what they do because of their religious authority system.

Recently there was a man in Boston, Massachusetts, who opened fire on a Planned Parenthood Clinic. Two people were killed because his religious authority system gave him permission to enact such violence. He was so adamant against abortion that he, in the name of God, killed other adults. Does that religious authority system make sense?

The entire world was stunned when a young Jewish man opened fire and killed the prime minister of Israel. This assassination was done in the context of a religious authority system. The killer has brazenly testified that he did it because he felt God wanted him to do it. Do you see that the problem with his actions and the actions of that Boston fanatic was really a problem with their reasoning about faith?

I'm afraid that in many mainline Protestant churches we have given people the impression that it doesn't matter what you believe, that one belief is as good as another, and that it doesn't really matter what church you go to as long as you go to church somewhere. In our effort to be tolerant and in our effort to be open— and we need to be both—we have lost a solid center about what we believe and why we believe what we believe. If it is true that people have gotten the message from our churches that religious authority really doesn't matter as long as people do what they feel is right for them to do, then we in mainline churches have some rethinking to do. Our need is not to become rigid fundamentalists; instead, what we need to rediscover is a theological center in our lives that makes sense and utilizes the Bible in a way that affirms life.

I want to make the claim that religious authority *does* matter. It does matter how you feel about your faith, how you talk about your faith, and how you reason about your faith. It matters. There's room for diversity, to be sure. And tolerance should be a part of our experience because tolerance is an expression of love. But I think a person can be open to the viewpoints of others and still be centered in his or her religious authority system. It is important for every Christian to take seriously the call to understand his or her faith.

Let's say one of your friends comes up to you and says, "I don't think your church is a good church because you have women who serve as elders. Why, you even have a woman at your church who is a minister! A minister! The Bible says women are supposed to learn in silence, that men are supposed to lead the church, and that women are supposed to take care of their children and support their husbands. I think your church is wrong!"

Obviously, that friend of yours has drawn some clear conclusions because of his or her religious authority system. What do you say to that friend? *Is* your friend right? *Is* your church displeasing to God because you believe women and men are equal citizens in the household of God? *Is* it the case that your friend believes the Bible more than you? *Is* your friend more of a Christian than you are because he holds such strong beliefs? What does *your* religious authority system say?

What if another friend says, "Because you have been divorced you have displeased God. And even though you are now happily remarried in your second marriage, you are really living in adultery. I'm afraid that, according to the Bible, if you were to die today, you would go to an eternity separated from God called hell. I'm sorry I have to tell you these things. But because I'm a Christian and because I really love you as a friend, I feel it is my duty to tell you the truth." What do you think of that religious authority system?

What would you say to a friend who has just shared this wonderful message from God with you? I'm afraid I might say, "It's been nice knowing you!" But do you see that your friend sincerely believes what she is saying to you and the reason she believes it is because of the religious authority system she is using.

What you believe and how you respond to these ideas will depend upon the clarification of your religious authority system. This is the task of every Christian—to understand what you believe and why you believe what you believe.

These two examples are not theoretical illustrations. On each Sunday that I preach in Louisville, within a few miles of my church there are other churches having worship services and Sunday school classes. At those churches, people hear exactly what I have used for examples. I have had church members from my congregation who have heard those very words from other Christians, who told them explicitly that they are not really Christians. When some people hear these ideas, they feel sheepishly guilty. They begin to feel badly about themselves because, after all, they think, "I really do deserve it. I probably am a bad person. I don't know the Bible as well as my friend seems to know it. Why, she can even quote the Bible. Maybe she is right."

Some people go into an emotional tailspin and never consider religion again. Some disagree. Others are confused. Still others think that because they heard this message in a church, it must be true—even though inside their hearts it doesn't quite seem right. Almost all of us have a person in our family who has tried to convince us that we are wrong religiously. One friend of mine dreads holidays because he is certain to be accosted by his sister-in-law about his religion. Are these bad people? No. Are they sincere people? Yes. Do I agree with the religious authority system they are using? Absolutely not. Yet, that's what I want to try to clarify. *What kind of religious authority system makes sense and is true to the gospel of Jesus Christ?*

I want to suggest that every balanced religious authority system has three dimensions—*Lights! Camera! Action!*

Lights! When I say *Lights!* I mean *personal spiritual experience with God.* Part of the presence of God is mystery. It's interesting that most Americans report they have had religious experiences, but most are reluctant to talk about those experiences. Religious experience needs to be a part of our religious authority system. Maybe that should really be the beginning place. After all, before there was a Bible to read there was the presence of God that people could experience in all its mystery and wonder. *Lights!* is that dimension of our Christian life where we feel close to God, where we experience God, where God touches something deep within our souls. *Lights!* is beyond an easy rational explanation. *Lights!* is the "aha!" *Lights!* is the quiet "yes" we feel standing in the Colorado Rockies as we feel closer to God than we've ever felt in our lives. A good friend of mine, Nick, just got back from British Columbia. He exclaimed to me over the phone, "I've never seen anyplace so beautiful. I mean it was *religious!*" Of course it was. There, in that extraordinary landscape, he had a *Lights!* experience.

On Christmas Eve I especially feel the presence of God. Christmas Eve is for me the most sacred moment in the entire church calendar; it is where I experience the holy. One year, after I had finished my sermon at the Christmas Eve service, the choir immediately began singing the "Hallelujah Chorus" from Handel's *Messiah.* I don't think I've ever felt music move me, inspire me, fill me, or touch me as much as that music did that night. Even as I write about that experience, the memory floods back, and I feel a sense of wonder and awe. I remember wanting to laugh and cry all at once!

One of the members of the choir said, "We heard you singing along." I did want to sing along because the music ushered me into a participatory experience with the presence of God. I didn't want merely to stand and listen. I wanted to sing to God. I wanted to reach out and hold God and to be held by God. I was part of a choir that has existed throughout the ages of the Christian faith. It was a moment of *Lights!*

And in that moment of Christmas Eve holiness, I didn't feel a need to explain the virgin birth of Jesus or complete an exhaustive study of the historical-critical information surrounding the biblical birth narratives. I didn't need to sort out what in American Christmas celebration is pagan and what is Christian and what is just plain old-fashioned holiday tradition. In that moment, in the glow of Christmas Eve, in the beauty of the sanctuary, surrounded by people I love and who love me, with candles burning and music filling my heart, I knew God was with me. I knew it because I *experienced* it to be so. The great poet Kabir put it like this—"I say only what I have seen with my own eyes . . . and you keep quoting the Scriptures!" Experience is essential to the life of faith.

As a young man, the psychologist Carl Jung had a dream of a great beautiful cathedral. Yet, the cathedral was smashed from above. Completely destroyed. When Jung awoke he understood the dream as a sign that what he needed more than anything in his life was direct, immediate experience of God. Not just talking about God, which churches tend to do a lot, but experience with the Divine. The rock singer Van Morrison says it well when he sings, "When will I learn to live in God?"

We need to learn to listen to religious experience. There's a very good reason why I believe women should share leadership in the church with men. It's because I experience women in the church as talented and gifted and passionate persons for God. My experience of that reality tells me it is true. I believe that women should take their place with men in the call of ordained ministry. I believe it, not simply because of the Bible, but because in my life experience one of my best friends is the Reverend Diane Zehr, and I have seen her call to ministry authenticated again and again as she exercises her gifts of ministry in various church settings. I have seen people such as Patricia Tucker Spier lead my denomination in the area of global mission. She has a marvelous competence. I have on my staff right now women who have wonderful skills, who possess an incredible spiritual capacity, and who over and over again express some of the most authentic ministry I have ever seen.

I also think people who have been divorced should be given full access to the life of the church. It's not because I'm liberal. It's not because I don't stand for traditional family values. On the contrary, it is because in my daily interaction with people I experience divorced persons as Christ-loved, Christ-forgiven, Christ-inspired. I see divorced persons—some remarried, some remaining single—who worship God each week, lead the church, sing in the choir, teach Sunday school, and, in many respects, live their faith better than I live my own. These are the experiences that continue to shape my life and faith. I suggest that part of a balanced, sensible, and gospel-inspired religious authority system should be the genuine listening to the authentic experiences of our lives.

In our reflection text, it is important to notice that Jesus did not have this personal and intimate experience with the living God

by sitting in a classroom studying the Bible or by attending a seminary class trying to figure out a correct belief, though I would add
that sometimes such study can glitter with ecstasy and joy. For
Jesus, his moment of the Spirit came through experience. Being
baptized is experience! The Spirit's coming is experience! Feeling
water drip off your body and feeling your soul encounter ecstasy is
experience! Experience is part of the ongoing movement with God.
That's *Lights!*

Camera! By *Camera!* I mean those *snapshots of religious life
that we find in the Bible.* That's what the Bible is—a kind of photo
album of how people searched for God, found God, lost God,
struggled for God, praised God, disappointed God. The Bible is a
scrapbook of how the Jewish people and the Christian people experienced God.

The Bible is not a divine rule book that dropped down from
the sky. The Bible is not a strict history book telling you the story
of the human race from the beginning until the second century
C.E. The Bible is not a science book giving all the correct scientific information that has ever been discovered and accepted as
true. The Bible is not even a systematic theology book giving one
universal master plan of salvation or one coherent view of theology that can be found on every page. As much as some try to make
the Bible strict history or science or theology, it is just not what
the Bible is. Just as it would be wrong for me to take an Emily
Dickinson poem and judge it on the basis of whether it agrees
with quantum physics, it would be wrong for me to ask the Bible
to be something it was never intended to be.

Recently in my wife's Sunday school class the members were
talking about the thorny topic of abortion. This is no easy matter
to address. After talking for almost an hour one of the class members popped up and said, "Well, I think all the answers are in the
Bible. All we need to do is read the Bible." I appreciate her feeling
and respect for the Bible, but the truth is, she is trying to make the
Bible into something it is not—namely, a divine answer book.
The Bible is not an answer book, nor was it ever intended to be
such. And, the truth be told, the Bible doesn't have all the answers.

One way to think about this complex book we call the Bible
is that it is a *collage of snapshots* of how Israel struggled to live its

faith, how Jesus struggled to live his faith, and how the early church struggled to live its faith as its members followed Jesus. Snapshots. That's the Bible.

We need the Bible. We as Christians need to experience Bible study. Both in small groups with other Christians and individually, we need to discover the richness of the Bible. Sermons need to help us understand the Bible better. Sunday school classes should put us in touch with the Bible. For too long churches have just assumed that people knew the Bible and that folks have the right tools to read the Bible. I think many pastors in mainline churches are now realizing that we have an internal mission field. Not only do our folks not know the Bible, they don't know how to even begin reading the Bible. And if they don't know the Bible, they don't have the resources to grow and deepen their faith. No longer can the assumption be made that the church knows its own story. Indeed, there's work to be done.

The trouble with the Bible and religious authority is that there are some who think that the only way to include the Bible in their religious authority system is to take the snapshots of the Bible and follow them literally today. It's a kind of biblical literalism that I think ultimately damages the faith and does great injustice to the Bible itself. Never mind the fact that the Bible was written in a different time and a different culture and is filled with different values. Put aside the reality that the Bible was composed over an immense span of time by so many different people writing for so many different purposes. Some still try to take the words of the Bible and argue that we should do everything these words say. These people contend that if we will do so, God will be pleased with us, but if we don't do these literal words, God will be displeased with us.

There are many problems with using the Bible in this way. First of all, *which snapshots of the Bible are you going to apply to your life?* There are people who say: "We only follow the Bible. We just go by the Bible. We don't practice anything except what's in the Bible. We don't give any interpretation; we just do what the Bible says." These people actually are being selective about which snapshots of the Bible they are trying to reproduce and follow in our age.

One snapshot of the Bible says, "Sell everything you have and give to the poor." Should we follow that snapshot literally? It's in the Bible!

Another snapshot of the Bible says, "Dash the heads of the little children against the rocks." Is that snapshot for us? Does it apply literally to our age?

Still another Bible snapshot reads, "Treat your slaves fairly." Is that snapshot of slavery, the literal owning of people, a practice that the Bible endorses? Are we to follow that part of the Bible?

In the last chapter we saw the communal structure of the early church in the book of Acts. Is that a snapshot God expects us to duplicate at the beginning of a new century?

However, there's a second problem with applying biblical snapshots in a literal fashion to our religious lives. It is *the mistaken notion that knowing the Bible is the same thing as knowing God.* I could show you all kinds of pictures of myself. There's a baby picture of me in the bathtub. There's a picture my mother took of me on my first trip to the barbershop. There's my first grade picture with my stylish and, no doubt trendy, Hollywood burr haircut. There's a picture of me holding my first trophy from Little League. There's my high school graduation picture of me with long hair, looking like I couldn't decide whether I was going to be a flower child or a disco king. There are wedding pictures of me much leaner and with no gray hair. Pictures of me with my children, now looking less lean and with lots of gray hair. I have different pictures from different times of my life. Each picture is of me, but each one reflects only a small part of my life.

Now, you could look at all of those snapshots. You could study those pictures. You could ask questions about those pictures. You, no doubt, could learn a lot about who I am by simply spending a significant amount of time looking at those photographs. But do you see that looking at the pictures is not the same as knowing *me*? It's not the same as knowing my pain or feeling my joy or appreciating my dreams. The pictures are fine, but they're not the same as being in my presence and letting me enjoy you as a friend and having the feelings that flow between two persons. Those pictures are not the same as touching my skin, hearing me breathe, smelling my aftershave lotion. You can learn about me through these pictures, but my presence is always beyond them.

I believe the Bible gives us snapshots of God. I love looking at the pictures, studying the snapshots, comparing some of the photographs, but I always must keep in mind that having a personal relationship with God is not the same as looking at the pictures. God is bigger than the Bible! That is why we don't worship the Bible—though, in some churches, I wonder if there isn't a practice of bibliotry. We worship the One about whom the Bible teaches us. We don't follow a book; we follow someone who reveals to us a living God—Jesus Christ. We need the snapshots of the Bible, to be sure—but never apart from the personal experience of God's presence. Therefore, we need to have the Bible as part of our religious authority system but never solely for our religious authority.

Well, if *Lights!* is personal experience and *Camera!* is snapshots of the Bible, then what is *Action!*? I would say that *Action! is the essence of the good news revealed in the life of Jesus Christ.* The whole life of Jesus Christ is revelatory of God's outrageously good news, a message of love and acceptance of people, and the call of God for people to nurture the whole creation in a just and responsible way.

Several years ago British broadcaster and journalist Malcolm Muggeridge did a documentary on the life of Mother Teresa of Calcutta, India. For weeks he followed her into the poorest of the world's neighborhoods. He watched her kneel and pray with dying children. He watched her gently take wet cloths and place them on the foreheads of fevered bodies. He witnessed the power of her praying for persons, and in her every step he saw the power of love released into the world. What Muggeridge witnessed was a life deeply committed to the spirit and principles of Jesus Christ.

When Muggeridge returned to London he was so moved by Mother Teresa's life that he wrote a book that I have appreciated for years and often give as a gift to friends. The book is titled *Something Beautiful for God.* When the good news of Jesus Christ penetrates our heart, our whole life is to become something beautiful for God. In our relationships, in our families, in our treatment of strangers is an opportunity to allow something beautiful for God to shine in this world. But what is true of Mother Teresa was also true of Jesus Christ.

You look at his life, and you see something beautiful for God shining through Jesus. He healed a leper, and that very action became good news to all the sick and outcasts of ancient Israel. He cared for a woman caught in sexual sin, and that action revealed the good news that God is a God of acceptance. Jesus held a child in his arms, and that action revealed a God of ultimate tenderness. You mean God could indeed hold me when I feel like a motherless child? The answer shining through the life of Jesus is nothing but a yes! He cast out an evil demon and gave expression to a God of restoration and wholeness. Jesus even died on a cross, and that pivotal action revealed a God willing to suffer with all the suffering of the world. And through the action of Jesus' resurrection, God is revealed as a God of ultimate and eternal life. Something beautiful for God indeed! In Jesus' life is revealed again and again and again the essence of God. And it is that essence that needs to guide us, lead us, move us, and have authority over us.

Over the last years there has been a great deal of research into the historical Jesus. You may have heard of the Jesus Seminar, a group of scholars who have tried to explore in a critical way exactly what Jesus said and what Jesus did and did not do. What's interesting to me is that, although their research is interesting and important, they don't address the ongoing importance of the figure of Jesus in the lives of people. There are many definitions of a Christian, but a simple one says that a Christian is someone who is moved by the person of Jesus and attempts to imitate his life. Often such a definition seems too simplistic for our complicated world. But there is something insightful about asking the following question on a daily basis—"What would *Jesus* do?"

What intrigues me about our reading from Matthew's Gospel is that in the baptism of Jesus I see all three of these elements of religious authority—*Lights! Camera! and Action!* I see *Lights!* because the Holy Spirit came and enlightened Jesus' mission at a crucial moment in his life. It was for him a personal religious experience. I see *Camera!* because he submitted himself to a profound biblical act of being washed, a practice found in the history of Israel and in the life of the early church. And I see *Action!* because by receiving baptism he was saying to all those who are baptized, "I am with you!" That one affirmation of God's presence with people is the essence of God and the quintessential message of the good news. After all, who is Jesus if not "God with us"?

These three—*Lights! Camera!* and *Action!*—are the trio of religious authority that makes sense to me both in its content and balance. Not just experience alone. Not just the Bible alone. Not just the life of Jesus alone. But all three together—personal experience joined with the snapshots of the Bible connected with the essence of good news—become a religious authority system that can guide the church.

Now you may be wondering, "Why does all of this matter? What's the big deal?" I'll tell you why I think it's important. A day will come when someone will ask you a question about your faith. Maybe it will be a friend. Who knows? Maybe your son or daughter will ask you something about what you believe. Someday you will have to make a theological decision about how you will treat another human being who is different from you. Maybe that person will be of a different race, a different sexual orientation, or a different culture. A day will come when someone will make the inference that your church is not a good church because you don't believe the right way. What will you say? Will you just be ashamed that you don't know much about your church, or will you be able to say some bright, positive word about your congregation that means so much to you? Or, perhaps one day, in the desert of your own confusion or pain, you will ask the question, "Where is God?" These questions move beyond theory and touch us where we live.

When any of these defining moments comes to you, I would encourage you to turn to the trio of *Lights! Camera!* and *Action!* And in the midst of these three you will know the direction of God for your life. You are not alone. There are resources for you. Your religious authority system matters because your faith matters, and faith matters because its object and passion is God.

Maybe the most important word regarding the Bible is a simple one. *The Bible needs to be read.* We can talk about it. Hear sermons from it. Read about it. But finally, this marvelous and rich and complex book needs to be opened and read.

Rita Dove, the talented African-American poet, once visited her daughter's first-grade classroom. She could see the hesitancy of the children to pick up a book and begin reading. I think a lot of us are afraid of picking up a book, especially the Bible, and reading it. Her poem, *The First Book*, written for those children, seems especially relevant to those of us contemplating the reading of the Bible.

> *Open it.*
> *Go ahead, it won't bite.*
> *Well . . . maybe a little.*
> *More a nip, like. A tingle.*
> *It's pleasurable, really.*
> *You see, it keeps on opening.*
> *You may fall in.*
> *Sure, it's hard to get started;*
> *remember learning to use*
> *knife and fork? Dig in:*
> *you'll never reach bottom.*
> *It's not like it's the end of the world —*
> *just the world as you think*
> *you know it.*

QUESTIONS FOR REFLECTION AND DISCUSSION

1. What kind of religious authority system did you grow up with?
2. In your own words, what do the metaphors *Lights! Camera!* and *Action!* mean?
3. Why is it insufficient to claim that the Bible alone is the religious authority system of faith?
4. What has been one of the most important religious experiences of your life?
5. Can you name an incident from the Bible that you simply have a difficult time accepting as either true or applicable to your life?

II

PRAYER

4
WHAT
IS
PRAYER?

He was praying in a certain place, and after he had fin-
ished, one of his disciples said to him, "Lord, teach us to
pray, as John taught his disciples." He said to them, "When
you pray, say:

> *'Father, hallowed be your name.*
>> *Your kingdom come.*
>> *Give us each day our daily bread.*
>> *And forgive us our sins,*
>>> *for we ourselves forgive everyone indebted to us.*
>> *And do not bring us to the time of trial.'"*

And he said to them, "Suppose one of you has a friend, and
you go to him at midnight and say to him, 'Friend, lend
me three loaves of bread; for a friend of mine has arrived,
and I have nothing to set before him.' And he answers from
within, 'Do not bother me; the door has already been locked,
and my children are with me in bed; I cannot get up and
give you anything.' I tell you, even though he will not get
up and give him anything because he is his friend, at least
because of his persistence he will get up and give him what-
ever he needs."

Luke 11:1–8

I want to share with you what has been for me the most important discovery in my spiritual life over the last ten years. It is this: *The reason I pray is not primarily to get things from God as much as it is to enhance my relationship with God.*

Let's be honest about it. Most of us grew up with the idea that we pray in order to get things from God. That was and is our basic concept of prayer.

I know that concept well since that is what was taught to me by my parents and my Sunday school teachers and, more broadly, given to me by the general culture of my religious upbringing. For years I believed in this kind of prayer, a prayer life of getting and gathering, and I did my best to practice this type of prayer. The theological understanding behind this view of prayer was that God was the "man upstairs," distant and removed from the human experience and, reflecting the culture of my time, always imaged as a male. The assumption and hope was that God might come down to the earth, intervene in the normal course of events, and answer my prayers. If I wanted this "man-upstairs God" to do things for me here on the earth, I had better send my messages up to God in the form of prayer requests. And so, I prayed.

Viewed in this way, prayer becomes a kind of mail-order-catalog business. We look at our lives, we see what we want, we dial the heavenly home shopping network, and we place our order with God. And then we wait. And wait. And wait. Sometimes we get what we want, and when we do we assume God has filled the order exactly the way we requested. Though if we are truthful about it, we're never quite sure if God actually answered our prayer or if we just got a lucky bounce and a coincidence rolled our way.

And, of course, sometimes we don't get what we want, and that perplexes us even more. Occasionally it even rattles our faith like a plane hitting a patch of turbulence. We pray for a sick friend, but our friend dies. We pray for a job, but we don't get it. We pour our sincerity and passion into those prayers, but we still come up empty.

In both experiences—getting what we want and not getting what we want—the basic understanding of prayer is the same. It's sending up messages to a distant God and then waiting for God to intervene in the world in order to give us what we want.

I think it's important to realize that treating prayer like a call-in order to the Home Shopping Network can quickly become ridiculous. I had a friend in college who tried to convince me that he prayed and prayed and prayed, and God eventually gave him exactly what he had been praying for—a brand new, bright yellow, high performance convertible sports car! He literally believed the words of Jesus—"Ask and you will receive." He had asked for a sports car, and he believed that God literally intervened in the world and came down to give him a sports car.

I had a parent tell me that every time her son goes to the plate in a Little League game she prays for her son to get a hit. She believes that God literally will intervene in the game and direct the bat in such a way as to make solid contact with the ball. I don't know what God does when another mother is praying for the pitcher.

I know people who, when the University of Kentucky plays the University of Louisville in basketball, actually pray for the Kentucky Wildcats to win. It's hard to believe, but it's true! The trouble is, I know that sitting on the opposite side of the arena are people praying just as hard and sincerely for the U of L Cardinals to win. Do these prayers cancel out each other like votes on election day? Or does this bring us to an age-old theological question—Does God wear a University of Kentucky blue sweatshirt or a University of Louisville red sweatshirt? I suspect Rick Pitino and Denny Crum might have differing theological positions on this matter. (Personally, I still suspect that God wears the cream and crimson of Indiana University!)

When I was in high school and went to the free-throw line in a close basketball game, I would sometimes pray for God to intervene in the situation and help me make the free throw so that my team could win. However, by the looks of my career shooting percentage, it's pretty apparent that God didn't pay much attention to my prayers! My prayers were sincere, but is that what prayer is all about?

All of this may sound pretty silly, but do you see the theological issue at stake? Is God up in heaven giving out sports cars? Is that how God works in the world? Is it the business of God to intervene in the world to make sure that baseball bats hit baseballs? Is it finally God who controls the outcome of basketball games? Is this how God works in our great big world? When I was in high school did God actually come down, intervene in the universe, and change the flight of one of my free throws so that the ball could go into the basket and let my team win? Is that what God's all about?

In our reflection text we read about the disciples who came to Jesus one day because they wanted to talk about prayer. Did you notice their opening question? They said, "Lord, teach us to pray the way John the Baptist taught his disciples to pray." Interesting. Evidently, John the Baptist had given his disciples a kind of identifying prayer, a prayer that when said would define the person praying as one of John's disciples. This prayer had become something of a spiritual bumper sticker or a club tattoo indicating, "*We* belong to John the Baptist." And that's exactly what the followers of Jesus wanted. "Give us a tattoo, Jesus, a kind of prayer that belongs to us and us alone. Give us a prayer that when we use it everyone will be impressed that we are your disciples. Give us a prayer that will show all the world where we stand!"

Notice, *they* wanted to talk about prayer at one level. *Jesus* wanted to move them gently to another level. *They* wanted to focus on the identifying words, the defining style, the impressionable features of a "Jesus prayer." *Jesus* wanted them to discover the deepest meaning of prayer which is to focus on relationship with God. Masterfully, Jesus did give them a prayer. But more than simply giving them a prayer to repeat, Jesus opened up a new vista for their understanding of God.

Fascinating, isn't it, that the beginning point of a deeper prayer life, at least according to Jesus, is at the place of a more meaningful theology? Jesus knew theology mattered. One of the most unfortunate developments in the church today is that many Christians seem to think theological thinking is for a limited group of professionals. On the contrary, what we think about God, how we talk about God, and the ideas we hold about God are crucial to our daily spiritual lives.

Several years ago I used to write a lot of poetry. I thought my poems were pretty good, but I had never had a critical evaluation of them. I called a literature professor from one of the local universities, and we had lunch together. I showed her some of my poems, and she was very gentle with me. She carefully read the poems. Finally she said, "You know, sometimes, before we write, we must learn to listen." She could have said, "This is the worst drivel I've ever read in my entire teaching career!" But she didn't. She would have been right, but she didn't. Instead, she wanted me to find a new level, a deeper level in the writing process.

The disciples wanted to talk about prayer at one level; Jesus moved them to another level. Jesus said, "When you pray, say, 'Father....'" The trouble with most of us is that we're so conditioned to call God "Father" that the original sense of wonder and surprise of addressing God in this way has been lost. To us it's no big deal. But for those early disciples—at that point in history and in that particular culture—to be able to address God in such a wonderful, intimate, endearing way was nothing short of a theological revolution. Jesus was suggesting that if you can imagine a warm, loving father holding a child in his strong arms, then you can imagine something of what God is like. In recent years biblical scholars have concluded that this image of Father was not necessarily original with Jesus, but was utilized by other religious leaders. Regardless, the whole point of this dialogue about prayer was to move the disciples to a deeper level of appreciation and experience of God.

Jesus was not saying that God is a male any more than Jesus would say that God is a female. Both masculine and feminine images of God can be found in the Bible. There are places in the Bible where God is imaged with breasts wanting to nurse a child or as a lover waiting for her spouse to come back home. Many images of God can be found in the Bible that are neither male nor female. God is a rock. God is a fortress. God is a mountain. Sometimes animal images of God are used. God is eagle. These are mere images, potent, of course, but still images. To literalize any of them would be a theological mistake. Jesus is not saying that the only way to address God is as father. Instead, he is offering an image of God that might open up inside those early disciples like a great eagle and then help them soar closer to God.

Frequently people in the church become confused over the issue of gender references to God. I had a woman just a few days ago ask me, "I heard one of our associate ministers refer to God as a woman. Do you think God is a woman?" And before I could even respond she continued, "I like to call God 'Father,' and I don't want to change!"

Her concerns were real and important to her. I tried to explain that in the Bible there are several images of God. I suggested that to say God is only male or only female is to make a mistake. What the church needs to do is use the full range of God images found in the Bible, as well as to discover new images in our contemporary culture that will bring us closer to God. My own denomination, the Christian Church (Disciples of Christ), has recently published a new *Chalice Hymnal*. In my estimation, the great strength of this hymnal is the variety of God images that can be found in it. I tried to assure the woman that no one was plotting to take away her primary image of "father," but that as an important option for her developing faith, she might consider discovering a variety of images of God.

The disciples who lived in the inner circle with Jesus were given this kind of familiar, intimate image to enhance their relationship with God in such a radical way.

"You mean to say, Jesus, that we can call God 'Abba' (the Aramaic word for papa, daddy, or dad)?"

"You mean to say, Jesus, that we can imagine God's being close and tender and loving?"

"You mean to say, Jesus, that we can have a relationship with the divine being that is as personal as a dad holding hands with his daughter as they take a walk on a fall afternoon?"

"Yes," says Jesus, "that's exactly the kind of God I am giving you!"

I can only imagine how the hearts of those early disciples started to brighten—the way stars come out at night, one at a time, piercing the night sky with light. Jesus wasn't giving them a little bedtime prayer; he was giving them a whole new way of thinking, of feeling, of imagining the presence of God in their lives.

The gift of prayer is a gift of relationship with God that is closer to us than the breath on our lips. This radical theological gift moves the disciples to the next level. Prayer, according to Jesus, is really about relationship. It's not about saying the right words.

It's not about getting all the right things from God. In fact, it's not *getting* at all. It is ultimately about being in a right relationship and enhancing that relationship.

Now, to help the disciples catch this spirit of relationship and prayer, Jesus told a story. Stories have the power to draw us in and invoke the imagination, as well as open up new worlds of being within our souls. Most of us are better with stories than we are with systematic theology.

The scene is familiar. Someone you knew in college stops by your house at midnight and wants to spend the night. He just knew you would love to see him as he was passing through town. In addition to the inconvenience of it all, he tells you that he hasn't eaten since noon and is starved. You go to the fridge, but it's empty. You go to the pantry, but all you have left is a little peanut butter and a can of Campbell's split pea soup. The stores are all closed.

So you decide to go to your next-door neighbor's for a little help. You knock at their door. No answer. You ring the doorbell. Still no answer. You even peck on their bedroom window. Finally, one of your neighbors comes to the door. You say, "Excuse me. Were you asleep?" Your neighbor, who is such a nice guy when he is out mowing his yard, is not amused. He's slow. Reluctant. Confused about what's going on. But finally he starts to get the picture.

You ask for food. He goes to the kitchen. He comes back with a sack full of groceries. Let the party begin! A few minutes later your house is full of friends, and the clatter of the midnight buffet fills the air. In spite of the inconvenience of the unexpected company, you have responded in the best way possible, and friendship finally has outweighed inconvenience.

The point of this little parable is a bit tricky, but it seems to be that *if even a drowsy, reluctant, hesitant neighbor finally responds to your persistent request, how much more will God respond and love and care and feel your deepest needs?* Does that mean God will give us everything we ask for when we pray? No. And for that we all probably should be grateful. It simply means that God is ever ready, ever open, ever responsive, ever receptive to be in relationship with us. Or, to put it more simply, God is better to us than even our best neighbor!

I have come to believe that Jesus may want to take our childhood concept of prayer, which is primarily a way of getting things from God, and move *us*, like the disciples, to a deeper level, a more spiritual and relational level. Not prayer as *getting*, but prayer as *enhancing relationship*. This infuses mystery into prayer. Prayer then becomes a way of experiencing the wonder and awe of God. Prayer becomes pure love.

If you've ever vacationed at the Grand Canyon or on some island in the Bahamas, you've probably seen couples who hold each other. They just stand and stare at the beauty of the place. It's as if a spell of magic has been cast over them, and, in some ways, that's exactly what has happened—magic and wonder. They now feel so close, so together. They feel that nothing could ever break them apart. And they also have that delicious feeling of never wanting this time to end. That's what prayer is about. It's about having time to embrace God, never wanting the time to end, feeling that our relationship with God will never end.

I don't know any celebrities, but my guess is that most celebrities are the loneliest people in the world. They always are surrounded by people, but they are deeply lonely because the people who hang around them typically want something from them. I wonder, for example, how many real friends Michael Jordan has. How does a president or a senator ever know who his or her friends are? I was in a piano bar in Carmel, California, once and in walked Clint Eastwood. It was a fun sight to see. And, my oh my, did the women come up to him in order to get a closer view! But as I watched him try to find a chair so he could enjoy the music, I started to feel sorry for him. Does he ever know who his friends are? When you are a celebrity, do you ever really know who loves you? What's missing with many celebrities is genuine, authentic relationship.

Do you think God ever feels lonely like that?

What would happen to our spiritual lives if, first of all, we stopped thinking of God as this absent God way up in the sky who drops in only for a few interventions, and started thinking of God as a divine friend who lives inside us every day? This is the companion who never leaves. What would happen?

What would happen to our lives if we stopped thinking of prayer as a mail-order-catalog operation and started thinking of prayer as a way of opening our souls to God? As a way of bringing to consciousness the divine being who is already with us at every moment of our lives? How would that begin to change us?

What would happen to our lives if we stopped thinking of prayer as asking, taking, and getting and started thinking of prayer as thanking God, as opening ourselves up to the divine presence, as a time of pausing to experience the wonder of God, as an intentional time to enjoy the companionship of God? What would our faith feel like then?

What would happen if we stopped thinking of prayer as formal address to God and started being playful and creative with our feelings toward God? Maybe we could start keeping a prayer diary. Maybe we could go out each morning and sit on our patio and greet the sun and pray with our hands stretched out to the sky. The neighbors may think we're a little strange, but so what? What if we started using special prayer music? Bach would be nice. But what about the group Acoustic Alchemy? Van Morrison? I still find some of the old Beatles music highly prayerful.

And here's the biggie! What would happen if we stopped thinking of prayer primarily as our communicating with God and started understanding prayer as listening, listening to the depth of our own soul, listening to the suffering and joy of our neighbor, listening to the voice of God? What would that experience of prayer do to our spiritual lives?

Please don't get the impression that I think it is wrong to share with God our hopes and dreams, our wants and desires. That's part of who we are, and we need to share that part of our lives with God. But primarily, *primarily,* the meaning of prayer is not to get, attain, achieve, and accomplish. Prayer is, I think, finally the practice of being in the presence of the Presence.

I have a circle of friends who are important to me. I enjoy these people. I like to spend time with them, talk to them, just be around them. I don't try to get things from these friends, nor do I try to use them. They are friends. I also know that relationships have to be nurtured. And so, even though they are busy and I am busy and even though we are separated by many miles of geography, I know that conscious effort has to be made to keep the friendship real. Relationships that mean anything at all demand something from us.

Roger Merrill tells the story of a friend who was getting ready to move into a new house. The friend met with a landscape professional and told him, "I want beautiful gardens all around the house, but I travel a lot and I'm not home much. I want automatic sprinklers. I want everything to be low maintenance. I want you to use every timesaving device possible." The landscaper listened for a long time and finally said, "Sir, I understand what you are saying. But before we go any further I think there is one thing you need to deal with. If there's no gardener, there's no garden."

Indeed, our relationship with God is like a garden. The poet Antonio Machado has written beautifully and poignantly about the garden of our lives:

> *The wind one brilliant day called*
> *to my soul with the odor of jasmine.*
> *"In return for the odor of my jasmine,*
> *I'd like all the odor of your roses."*
> *"I have no roses; all the flowers*
> *in my garden are dead."*
> *"Well then, I'll take the withered petals*
> *and yellow leaves and the waters of the fountain."*
> *The wind left. And I wept. And I said to myself:*
> *"What have you done with the garden that was entrusted*
> *to you?"*

I believe that prayer becomes our way to cultivate, at a conscious level, our relationship with God; it's our way of taking care of our spiritual garden. We pray, not just when we need something, not just when we are in trouble. But we pray, taking time to speak and listen to the divine friend. It's the relationship that finally matters. Like in a garden, there is joy, food, and beauty. And that's the gift Jesus was giving the early disciples, and that's the gift given to all of us—the beauty of relationship.

So pray, knowing that each day is sacred. Pray, knowing that God is within you. Pray, knowing that God is a friend to you. Pray, knowing that God always hears you. Pray, knowing that all prayer is ultimately love. Pray, knowing that you say "yes" to God and God says "yes" to you.

The key is getting started. Not just talking about prayer, or reading about prayer. Begin finding your quiet moments—and pray.

QUESTIONS FOR REFLECTION AND DISCUSSION

1. What concept of prayer did you receive as a child?
2. How we imagine God is important to how we pray. What are some images of God that touch your soul?
3. Can you recall a moment in your life when you felt close to God, but you weren't literally praying? A time when you felt as if you were in a prayerful state, but you weren't actually saying a prayer?
4. What puzzles you most about the biblical story of the next-door neighbor who goes and knocks on the door at midnight?
5. If prayer isn't primarily designed to get things from God, then why pray?

5

How Does
GOD
Answer My
PRAYERS?

*"So I say to you, Ask, and it will be given you; search, and
you will find; knock, and the door will be opened for you.
For everyone who asks receives, and everyone who searches
finds, and for everyone who knocks, the door will be opened.
Is there anyone among you who, if your child asks for a
fish, will give a snake instead of a fish? Or if the child asks
for an egg, will give a scorpion? If you then, who are evil,
know how to give good gifts to your children, how much
more will the heavenly Father give the Holy Spirit to those
who ask him!"*

Luke 11:9–13

I recently read a collection of prayers offered by children and
found some of them rather insightful.

One little boy named Bruce wrote, "Dear God, please send
me a pony. I never asked for anything before. You can look it up!"

A little girl named Joyce prayed, "Dear God, thank you for
the baby brother, but what I prayed for was a puppy."

One ten-year-old prayed, "Dear God, can't you make church
more fun? What about having a few videos?"

Nan wrote a prayer to which many of us can relate: "Dear
God, I bet it's very hard for you to love all the people in the world.
There are only four in our family, and I can never do it!"

Children also have a more serious side. In their prayers are revealed some very adultlike questions about life. Eight-year-old Daniel, for example, prayed, "Dear God, I love you because you give us what we need to live, but I wish you would tell me why you made it so we have to die."

In some ways all our prayers to God are childlike. We reach out to God. We want things from God. We want God to do things for us. The trouble is, as adults, the urgency of our prayers becomes more intense. It's one thing to ask God for a pony. But it's another thing, isn't it, to pray to God for a sick child or a dying parent or an alcoholic husband?

How does God answer prayer?

Several years ago the entire state of Kentucky was touched deeply by a tragedy. A youth group from the Church of God in Radcliffe, Kentucky, was on its way home from a day at King's Island amusement park. These were kids like your kids and my kids. These were kids who went to church every Sunday, sang in the youth choir, and attended Sunday evening youth group events. These were kids trying to do the right thing in their lives as they were growing up.

They had a wonderful day at King's Island. The rides. The junk food. The laughter. That night when they got on the church bus a youth leader raised his hand, and all the kids became quiet. They knew what to expect next. This was prayer time. I wasn't on that bus, but I've been on buses like that and led prayers like that. I can imagine the prayer sounding almost childlike: "Dear God, give us a safe trip home. . . ."

However, it was not a safe trip home.

The church bus was traveling down Interstate 71 near Carrollton, Kentucky. Headlights of a pickup truck approached the bus like an out-of-control rocket. Before the bus driver even understood what was coming at them, the bus had been hit. The gas tank ruptured. Flames exploded against the black sky. And that night the entire state of Kentucky was shaken to its core with grief. Twenty-four wonderful, vibrant, beautiful young people were killed and three adults also. Life was needlessly and senselessly snuffed out. The driver of the pickup truck was drunk.

How does God answer prayer?

That's not just a theoretical question, is it? It's really a question about how God works and operates in this world. It perhaps is the biggest and most difficult theological question to be faced. *Does* God answer prayer? Does God *respond* to prayers that are offered sincerely, genuinely, and meaningfully? What about those times in our lives when we've prayed for a loved one to get well or for a marriage to get back together or for a desperately needed job to open? What about those times when we've prayed and prayed and prayed and still our loved one did not get well, the marriage fell apart anyway, and the job went to someone else? What about *those* times?

How does God answer prayer?

I want to suggest that there are basically *two views of God* in our world. One view—and it's the one most commonly accepted by Christians—understands God as the *great controller of the universe.* The other view of God—which also is a Christian perspective but not as commonly held—is of *God as caring friend and companion of the world.*

If you can imagine God's sitting behind a great computer console and pushing buttons for the events of this world to happen, then you can begin to understand God as the great controller. I recently saw a page from a friend's "Far Side" calendar. This particular page showed God in heaven staring at a computer screen, a maniacal look on his face, his fingers poised at the computer keyboard. On the screen was a man on earth, casually walking down the street, minding his own business. However, above his head was a baby grand piano tied perilously to a rope about ready to be dropped on top of the man. The caption of the illustration simply read, *"God at work on his computer."* Funny? Funny, I suppose, if you're not the man walking under the piano! The trouble is we've all walked under the piano from time to time, haven't we? And if we haven't, then someone we love has.

Maybe God has a promotion button that God presses for you. Maybe God had a lottery button for that couple in Arizona who recently won millions of dollars. Maybe God has a NCAA championship button for some college basketball team. Maybe God has a World Series winning team button. Is it the case that God has "good" buttons to push for the universe?

And maybe—here is the other side of this sticky theological problem—maybe God has a dark side. Does God push "bad" buttons too? Does God have a viciously mean side? Maybe God has a cancer button or a heart attack button or a blindness button or a crippling arthritis button. Maybe God has a button for earthquakes and hurricanes and Midwestern tornadoes. And maybe, just maybe, God has a church bus accident button. Is this the kind of God we worship each Sunday? Is this the God of the Christian faith?

My guess is that most of us in one way or another have wrestled with the puzzle of how God works in the world. If you believe in God as the great controller of the universe, that means you believe that every detail of every action of every day has happened in the world because it was God's will.

But that's a problem, isn't it?

It's a problem because if God is causing church buses to be hit by drunk drivers, then that kind of God is a madman or a lunatic. That kind of God is not worthy of our worship. Why, even we as human beings know that causing such tragedies is wrong and should not be tolerated. People who blow up a bus in Jerusalem or a pub in Northern Ireland should be prosecuted. We know that about earthly criminals. How, therefore, can we worship a God who causes such events to happen? Surely God is not exempt from the fundamental principles of justice and compassion we as human beings hold to be true.

Most of us sidestep a little with our theology at this point and say, "Well, it's not that God *causes* these things to happen. It's just that God *lets* these things happen." But think about it. If one of my children were about to be hit by a car and I had the power to stop that accident from happening, but I don't stop it from happening, isn't that just as bad as if I had pushed her or him out in front of the car in the first place? Saying that God *caused* a bus accident to happen and saying that God *let* a bus accident happen when God could have stopped it are actually saying the same thing. There's no difference.

And so we do a "theological Texas two-step" once more and go in a slightly different theological direction. We say, "Well, even though the bus accident *looked* like a tragedy and even though it *looked* like an evil thing for a drunk driver to kill twenty-four children, it's not *really* a bad thing because God is going to accomplish a greater good through this event. God's ways are above our ways, and, besides, the kids who were killed in that fiery crash got to go to heaven anyway." Yes, I have heard this kind of reasoning. Certainly there are sincere Christian people who understand God in this way, and I would never try to diminish the sincerity of their faith.

Yet, do you hear how hollow that kind of theological reasoning sounds? That theology is saying there is no evil in the world, no real tragedy in this life, no bad things. And although many sincerely try to live with this understanding of God, in the end, it clearly is not intelligible.

The Holocaust that killed more than six million Jews was not really a tragedy; it just looked like it from our limited human perspective. The bombing of Pearl Harbor, which shook our nation to the core and propelled World War II into the depths of human loss, just appeared to be a tragic event. The atrocities going on in Bosnia are really good things that just appear to us as bad things. The murder of two lovely children in a South Carolina town by a pathologically ill mother just looked like a bad thing. The painful divorce of a couple is just an illusion. And the inferno crash of a church bus full of young people was really God's way of accomplishing a greater good.

I cannot agree with this theological explanation. To me, it makes no sense to say that God causes bus crashes, that God lets them happen, that God lets them happen in order to accomplish some greater good written in the cosmic blueprints found only in the mind of God. I have to be honest with my faith and honest with God, and for me it just doesn't make sense. One important dimension of faith is having a faith that finally adds up and is at least credible.

I want to be careful here because I would never deny that good can come out of tragedy. I have seen that again and again. Some of the people I admire most in this world are people who have endured tragedy and have grown through the most difficult of circumstances. Even the apostle Paul writes about "suffering developing character." But to say that good can come out of tragedy is not the same as saying that God *causes* tragedy in order to accomplish good.

Those kids on that church bus prayed to God as they pulled away from the King's Island parking lot. They prayed sincerely, "God, give us a safe trip home. . . ." Did God ignore their prayer? Did God refuse to answer their prayer? Is it the case that sometimes God answers "yes" and sometimes "no" to prayers? And when do you know the difference between God's "yes" and God's "no"?

Maybe this is what happened on that awful night on Interstate 71. The problem with the prayer on the bus that night was that the person saying the prayer didn't believe enough, wasn't sincere enough, wasn't Christian enough. The reason the prayer wasn't answered was because of some flaw in the person who was praying. Sound ridiculous? As ridiculous as that sounds, that kind of human shaming and guilt dumping has taken place again and again in the guise of Christian theology.

Let me tell you about Sue Redman. I met Sue in the hospital room of one of my church members. She had cancer. I visited with her a little bit one day, but I could tell that she was troubled in a peculiar kind of way. We talked a little longer. As I got ready to leave her room, I said to her, "Would you like for me to say a little prayer with you today?" She said, "I guess so. The people in my church keep telling me that if my faith were stronger, God would heal me." And when those words dripped from her lips like a slow IV, she could not even look me in the eyes. Can you feel her shame? It wasn't enough that she was sick with cancer and in a fight for her very life, but she had church people telling her that God was not with her because she didn't have enough faith! At a time when she needed God the most, she was being told she wasn't good enough for God.

How does God answer prayer?

I want to suggest that we take our cue from Jesus in the reflection text. The disciples wanted Jesus to give them a prayer. Instead, Jesus gave them a theology. Isn't that the way it is with Jesus? We want easy steps, a quick solution, a fast fix. Jesus offers a way of life, a new orientation, a lifestyle.

"Suppose your daughter comes to you," says Jesus, "and she wants a chocolate chip cookie for dessert. Would you give her a poisonous rattlesnake? Or suppose your son comes to you and asks for a peanut-butter-and-jelly sandwich for lunch. Would you give him a deadly McScorpion to eat?"

Well, of course, we know the answer.

We as parents know how to relate to our children in good ways. We would never give them poison. We would never do anything to hurt them, because we love them and want the very best for them. The essential definition of a parent is someone who sacrificially works for the well-being of the child.

Jesus says, "If you parents who lose your patience, who fly off the handle, who get frustrated beyond words, who become so exhausted that you don't think you can change one more dirty diaper, if you parents *who are evil* know how to treat your children, how much more will God give you the *Holy Spirit* when you pray!"

And that's the answer! When we ask and seek and knock on the door of God, there is one answer God always gives. Actually, not so much an answer as a response, a singular response. God ceaselessly offers to all people who pray *the gift of the Holy Spirit.*

Don't let the language of the Holy Spirit throw you or frighten you. The Holy Spirit is God's breath, God's living energy, God's intimate friendship, God's daily companionship. Jesus is saying that when we turn to God in prayer, there is only one answer that we look for and count on and rely upon. It is the answer that says, "I am with you." This is the Christmas message, the Easter message, the Jesus message, the message of the church community. It is a message that says God is with us, and it is the answer that continues lifting and rolling upon the shores of our lives every time we pray.

How does God answer prayer?

If God is not the great controller of the universe, who exactly is God and what does God do in the world? The vision of God presented by Jesus is that of God as *caring friend and loving companion.* Friend! Companion! It's important to acknowledge that friends don't control friends. I cannot make a person be my friend. I cannot force someone to be my life companion. I cannot make my children be my friends. Friendship is chosen and bestowed always as a gift. When a person chooses to be our friend, it makes all the difference in the world and fills our lives with wonder and surprise.

Walter Winchell once said, "A real friend is one who walks in when the rest of the world walks out." That might be a pretty good way of describing God. God is the one walking into our lives when everyone else is walking out. The corporation may walk away from us—as many middle-class males are discovering as they are caught in the turbulence of corporate downsizing. Fame may take a hike—as most celebrities have discovered from time to time. Even people we have considered to be friends for years may decide to turn away from us. Just ask a woman who is recently divorced or a man who has suffered mental illness. Where are the friends at that time? But God is the one who always and forever is walking toward us, and the one who promises never to leave us.

God, however, cannot *make* you be a friend because if God *made* you be a friend then it would no longer be the choice and gift of friendship. God uses friendship power in the world, not controlling power. God uses the power of love, not the power of violence. God uses the power of invitation, not the power of coercion. God does have power in the world; that's undeniable. The central question becomes—What type of power does God use in our lives? That's the big question. And that is why I'm suggesting that God uses a different kind of power than the intervening and controlling power that most of us grew up believing God used.

This is why people may say, "Well, if God had wanted to stop that truck from hitting that bus, God could have done that."

And I say, "No! That's not how God operates in the world."

"Well," some suggest, "if God had wanted to stop the Holocaust from happening, if God had wanted to stop that plane from crashing, if God had wanted to stop that heart attack from killing my grandfather, God could have intervened in the world and stopped it from happening."

And again I say, "No! That's not the kind of power God uses in this world. That's not how God operates. God is present in the world. That's without a doubt. But the power of God in this world is the power of love! The power of God is not dictator power, but the power of persuasion, invitation, and companionship. God does use power in the world, but it is a special kind of power—friendship power!"

In ancient Greek tragedies the characters of the play would act upon the stage before wealthy audiences. As the plot would unfold, the play would become more and more of an impossible mess. When the plot became twisted and the characters miserable, the stagehands would mechanically lower a "god" character on the stage who would then sweep up the main character, thus saving the day and making everything OK in the nick of time for the play to end. This kind of god was called the *deus ex machina* (god from the machine)—the god lowered mechanically upon the world of the stage.

The God revealed by Jesus Christ is not the god lowered upon the stage of our lives, occasionally making guest appearances in order to stop heart attacks or divorces or bombs or car accidents. The God the Christian faith reveals is willing to live upon the stage of our lives in every single minute of every single day. That kind God is a caring friend and loving companion. In every high moment of our living experience, God is there. In every low moment of our lives, God is there. The caring friend supports us when we need strength, encourages us when we are down, and walks beside us when we have lost our way.

I had a very pious woman once tell me that she had secretly always wanted to go to New Orleans for Mardi Gras. But she explained, "I would want a hotel room with a balcony above the street. I don't really want to participate in it; I just want to stand on the balcony and watch it all." Although I think she really wanted to participate in the carnival of Mardi Gras more than what she was honestly saying, there is something about her image which calls for reflection. God is not standing on the balcony. God is not merely looking down on all the comings and goings of the world from a protected place. On the contrary, this God becomes flesh, as John's Gospel indicates, and dwells among us. And it is this friend and companion who always listens and responds to our prayers, not from above, but in the midst of life's carnival.

You may wonder as I have, *"Did God answer that prayer for that youth group that night on its way home from King's Island?"*

I believe the answer is yes.

First of all, I believe that God was with them. I think God was with them, bringing them together for a fun day. I think God was with them as they built fellowship with one another in the name of Christ. Yes, good things that happen are a sign of God's working presence. I also think God was with them even in the tragedy of their deaths. Was it God's will that a drunk driver hit that bus and killed those teenagers? Absolutely not! Does God want teenagers killed in car crashes? Never! God was more brokenhearted than anyone in the midst of that ordeal. There were many complexities to the situation. God was offering to the drunk driver better and more responsible behaviors; tragically, he turned away from God's options. People have the freedom to do that. His irresponsible use of freedom hurt the freedom of others. This is the nature of the world. I believe that God was with those teenagers to the very last moment of their lives and beyond. The whole idea of heaven is that God does not abandon us after we die. God was with the survivors too. God was with those families giving them comfort beyond any human words. And God was with that church as its members tried to pick up the painful pieces of their lives. Was it easy? No. But God was the ever-present companion and the constant friend who kept on encouraging, supporting, and giving the gift of inner strength.

I believe God answers all prayers. In fact, I think there is finally one answer to every prayer we have ever uttered or ever will utter. "Yes, my son. Yes, my daughter," God says. "I will be with you always."

I pray about a lot of things in my life, and I pray for a lot of people, but I know that all my prayers are answered because no matter what happens in life, God is with me. I pray for my children. I don't really know what will happen to them. The future is wide open. Both dangerous and exciting. And forever unpredictable. I want them to say, "Yes," to God's will and God's presence. I want them to be followers of Jesus Christ. I pray for them and want them to be safe, but there are no guarantees. Regardless of what happens to them, I know that my prayers are answered before I even pray, because the gift I have in Jesus Christ is the gift of God's ever-present Spirit.

And that presence is with you too. You too have probably said prayers over ordeals and situations that have brought you to your knees. One day you are strong and vital, the next day you are in a flimsy hospital gown undergoing prostate surgery. Is it cancer? Is it not? Will you be OK? You pray. And you should pray, because in that moment you need the flowing assurance that you are not alone, that God is with you, that you are held by an invisible friend. But you have had joys too. A daughter's wedding brings tears to your eyes. She is beautiful and, to top it all off, you even like the young man she is marrying! This is a rich moment. Full. Alive. And you are grateful for it, so you pray. Your prayer acknowledges that the unseen energy in the world that makes life worth living flows to you from the one who is the lover and friend of the universe. In sorrow and in joy, we pray.

No wonder one little girl named Nora prayed this simple prayer, "Dear God, I don't ever feel alone since I found out about you." Amen, Nora. You've got it! Amen.

QUESTIONS FOR REFLECTION AND DISCUSSION

1. Have you ever wondered about how God answers prayer? If so, what was going on in your life to make you ask the question?
2. What are the problems you see in understanding God as the "great controller" of the world?
3. Have you ever had a moment in your life when you have asked, "How could God have let this happen?" Describe the feelings around that time in your life.
4. Brainstorm a list of qualities we normally associate with the word *friend*. Why is the concept of friend an important way of understanding God?
5. Prayer is coming into the presence of God. Can you describe an experience in your life when you felt yourself in the presence of God?

6
HOW
DO I
BEGIN TO
PRAY?

O come, let us sing to the LORD;
let us make a joyful noise to the rock of our salvation!
Let us come into his presence with thanksgiving;
let us make a joyful noise to
him with songs of praise!
For the LORD is a great God,
and a great King above all gods.
In his hands are the depths of the earth;
the heights of the mountains are his also.
The sea is his, for he made it,
and the dry land, which his hands have formed.
O come, let us worship and bow down,
let us kneel before the LORD, our Maker!
For he is our God,
and we are his people of his pasture,
and the sheep of his hand.
O that today you would listen to his voice!
Do not harden your hearts, as at Meribah,
as on the day at Massah in the wilderness,
when your ancestors tested me,
and put me to the proof,
though they had seen my work.
For forty years I loathed that generation

> *and said, "They are a people whose hearts go astray*
> *and they do not regard my ways."*
> *Therefore in my anger I swore,*
> *"They shall not enter my rest."*

Psalm 95

When I say the word *prayer,* what mental picture comes to your mind?

We all have mental pictures of prayer. In the house where I grew up, there hung in the dining room a picture of an old bearded man with his hands folded, his head bowed, a loaf of crusty bread on the table. It was a picture of prayer. It was only years later when I became a minister that I found that same picture in literally hundreds of other houses. All along, I thought we were the only ones who had it! Not so. Mental pictures are good because they can open up a world of meaning for us. But sometimes our mental pictures are not so good because they limit us. Instead of helping us see, they block our sight. Vision can become limited.

What I would like to do is offer some mental pictures of *how to pray.* Having looked at the theology of prayer in the last chapters, I now want to talk about the actual experience of praying. These mental pictures are not the same as "three quick and easy lessons to a better prayer life." If only it were that simple! Instead, these are some ways I have learned to pray over the last years, and I share them with you in hopes that some or all of them might be helpful to you. These may be pictures you already have inside your mind. If so, that's great. Some of these pictures might be new for you. Most of all, what I want is for you to find ways of praying that really connect your soul to God. After all, that's what prayer is all about.

The first mental picture I would suggest is that of *praying as conversation.* This is the one mental picture that perhaps is the most familiar to us. We take time in the day to share our thoughts, our feelings, and our emotions with God. We can do this by sitting down, closing the door, and actually taking time to talk to God. We may have designated times, such as every morning or at bedtime. In the Catholic tradition there are "hours" of prayers—

designated times during the day when one should pray. These hours become the daily structures for monastic communities and their ministry of prayer. I think it's important to build into our lifestyles structured times to pray.

Sometimes people say to me, "Well, I just talk to God when I feel like it. I pray at any time I want because I know that God's always with me."

That's true. God is always with you. There's nothing wrong with having a casualness in prayer. At the same time, part of a healthy spiritual life is taking intentional time to "verbalize" our thoughts to God. Some people like to think their prayer to God. Some people have found it helpful to write prayers to God in a journal, like letters to a friend. Some people schedule in their day quiet time or meditative moments. Regardless of the method, prayers need to be expressed regularly to God.

Occasionally people who've not prayed much ask me, "How do I get started? What should I say to God when I start to pray?"

My answer is that you can say anything you feel, anything you think, anything you've always wanted to say to God. If you're scared, tell God. If you're angry, tell God. If you're joyful, tell God. A good rule of thumb on how to pray is—*Don't get hung up on how to pray!*

Praying is not the time to try to use all the right words, nor is it the time to deliver a Pulitzer-Prize type of prayer to God. You don't need to be literary or formal. Just begin thinking thoughts, talking thoughts, writing thoughts. Several books of prayers have been written that can be used in a meaningful way. I especially like some of the new prayer books that incorporate prayers from different cultures and religious perspectives. Just reading a prayer can become prayer.

Those of you who live with teenagers know that wonderful feeling when your teenager finally decides to talk to you. You might go for days with your teenagers, and they never really talk. Oh, there is an occasional grunt every now and then, but real talking and real sharing are rare. They might ask you for the car keys. They might ask you for money. (No, they *always* ask for money!) They might ask you to take them to the mall or pick them up after school. But genuine talking—the kind of talking when they sit down and tell you what's going on in their lives or what they're feeling—is as priceless as gold.

Real praying is like real talking to God. You begin by sharing your thoughts and feelings. It should never be forgotten that when you really talk and share life with another, it makes all the difference in the world. That's especially true of our connection with God.

Someone told me a joke about a man who walked into a pet store and said, "I want to return this talking bird."

The owner said, "Well, sir, we guarantee that all our birds can talk, but we can't guarantee *when* they will talk."

"No, no," the man said. "The bird talks all right, but I don't like its *attitude*. For six days I said to the bird, 'Can you talk?' The bird said nothing. Every morning and every night I stood in front of the cage and said, 'Can you talk?' The bird said nothing again. Finally this morning I lost my temper and shouted at the bird, 'You stupid bird, can you talk?!'"

"So, what happened?" the owner asked.

"That bird looked at me and said, 'Yeah, I can talk. Can you fly?'"

Well, one question regarding praying as conversation might be: I know you can *talk* to God, but can you *listen*? And that's the other part of conversational prayer. Some people call it meditation, and it's the most important part of conversational prayer. When we pray we need to discover the element of listening for God. Listening for the voice of God. And, in the process of it all, listening to our own lives.

I want to be careful here. I'm not suggesting that God is going to whisper literal words in your ears or that God is going to tell you exactly what you need to do for the day. Listening to God is not a direct A-to-B or 1-2-3 kind of linear experience. Prayer is mystery. Frankly, I become a little suspicious of people who glibly say in every other breath, "God told me to do this" or "The Lord led me to do that." I do think God speaks to us, but it's not like having a direct toll-free number. The voice of God is a metaphor that means we feel the presence of God moving us along in life when we pray.

In my personal experience with prayer, I get what I call insights, awarenesses, thoughts, feelings, or inklings about what I should do in my life. These insights or inklings are the ways God leads us in our lives. These after-prayer intuitions are signs of the presence of God. Indeed, these insightful moments have the power to transform us and the people for whom we pray.

One of the psalms reads, "Be still and know that I am God." That's listening. John Henry Newman speaks of prayer as "heart speaking to heart." That's listening to God. Thomas Merton wrote several years ago, "All prayer is finally listening." That's prayer as a listening relationship.

There have been many times in my life when I was so confused or so discouraged or so hurt that all I could do was pray. Have you ever had those times? Have you ever had those moments when you literally had nowhere else to turn but to God?

I remember so vividly the first time I received at my office an anonymous letter that absolutely ripped my ministry apart. I was twenty-four years old. I was so new in the ministry and so eager to please and make everyone happy. As I read that letter with its hurtful words and attacking attitudes, I was devastated. Today if I would get one of those letters I would just throw it away and go on with my life. But at that time, I didn't know how to handle it. I naively assumed everybody liked me!

What's utterly amazing is that after I closed the office door and prayed, the world did not seem so confusing or the difficult situation so impossible. Confusion gave way to clarity. It's as if God granted me a sense of calm or peace. At that moment I felt I heard the voice of God. It was not a literal, audible voice. I felt the presence of God with me at a very vulnerable time in my life.

In prayer we speak to God, but in prayer we also listen for God to say, "Come on. You can do it." "Hang in there. We can figure this out." "Don't worry so much. I'm with you." And that's what I heard that day. Before my time of prayer, I was ready to give up this entire vocation of ministry; after prayer I knew God was with me. Conversational prayer is both talking and listening.

Another way of praying is *praying as reading*. This involves the Bible. There are many effective ways you can read the Bible. You can read the Bible in order to understand it rationally. You can ask questions such as, "What does this passage mean?" "How does this passage relate to my life today?" "What does this Bible passage teach about this topic or that subject?" It's great to read the Bible like that. I tried in the first three chapters to suggest ways of reading the Bible that bring forth the gold of theological meaning. I love to study the Bible critically and rationally, and the church today cannot have too much of that kind of biblical exploration.

But there's another way of reading the Bible, and that is reading the Bible as an act of prayer. Sometimes people refer to this method of reading the Bible as devotional reading. In the tradition of spirituality this is called *lectio divina*, which simply means "reading for the divine word." This way of reading looks for the living Word to pop out of the many words of the text and connect spiritually with the reader.

How you do this is very simple. First, you read a passage of the Bible. It might be obvious, but I cannot say it too much—we finally have to make a little time and open up the Bible. Then, when you come across a phrase or even a word in the text that makes a soulful connection with you, you simply stop and repeat that phrase or word like a prayer. You repeat the word again and again and again. You let the phrase resonate inside you. You let the word echo within your soul. You listen, not with the rational part of your mind, but with the deep soul of your heart. You feel the passage. You taste the passage. You touch the passage. That's praying the Word.

Take our reading from Psalm 95 as a point of reflection. As you read this passage you can ask all kinds of questions about the background of the psalm, its relationship to us, critical historical information about the psalm, etc. And that information is not unimportant. (Bible commentaries and dictionaries can be helpful as we try to read the Bible with our rational self.) But you also can use a phrase in this psalm as an experience of prayer.

What caught my soul as I read the psalm was the expression *"in his hands are the depths of the earth."* Think of that. *"In his hands are the depths of the earth."* Have you ever felt your life was spinning out of control? *"In his hands are the depths of the earth."* Have you ever felt as if you didn't know what you should do next? *"In his hands are the depths of the earth."* Have you ever wondered how your family would survive a crisis? *"In his hands are the depths of the earth."*

It may feel a little awkward, but take a few moments and pray this now: *"In his hands are the depths of the earth."*

Again: *"In his hands are the depths of the earth."*

Pray it one more time: *"In his hands are the depths of the earth."*

Do you see what has happened? Suddenly a word or phrase has become a prayer. It speaks to us—not at a rational level, but at the level of the soul. Written words become prayers of our heart, sinking into our being and leaving an indelible stamp upon us. Repeating such prayers turns them into our mantras, words that continue inside our soul like little ringlets of water upon a glassy pond. Reading can become a sacred act of praying.

Another mental picture of prayer is *praying as ritual.* By ritual I mean doing ordinary actions that become extraordinary in their significance. In his book *Breakfast at the Victory* James Carse writes, "The highest achievement of the spiritual life is within the full embrace of the ordinary. Our appetite for the big experience— sudden insight, dazzling vision, heart-stopping ecstasy—is what hides the true way from us." It is the extraordinary in the ordinary that can become prayer. In the Buddhist tradition there is an expression, "Chop wood; carry water," which is a way of saying that spiritual meaning can be found in the smallest, most ordinary functions of the day.

It's really too bad that the word *ritual* has taken on such a negative connotation with some Christians. We need rituals. Rituals mark outwardly the experiences we have inwardly with God. When we do rituals we open our soul to the mystical resonance of the Christian life. Jesus often used the ritual of going to the desert to pray. The fact that he took time to go to the desert at all became for him a kind of prayer. Jesus had rituals, certain things he would do and certain places he would go to find spiritual renewal. He would go to the desert for the quiet, or he would go to the ocean to feel the ebb and flow of life. He would go to the mountains and sense the greatness of creation and Creator. And what he did was transform an ordinary place into a sacred cathedral of prayer. The desert isn't just a desert, it became his sanctuary. The seashore isn't just the seashore, it became his chapel. Invariably, he would go to one of his ritual places right before he would enter an intense period of life. Sometimes, *after* a difficult period of life he would go to his ritual places.

Often I write my sermons in my study at home. I almost always light a certain candle every time I write the sermon. In the winter I always have a fire going in the fireplace. It's a ritual. My dog sleeps in the chair a few feet away from my desk. Just the sheer act of lighting the candle is a prayer. Just starting a fire early in the morning before I write is a kind of ritual prayer that invokes the presence of God in my creative process. No words. No verbalizing. But the action connects me to God. In fact, the whole arrangement and feeling of the room is prayerful.

Not long ago I was at a wonderfully elegant dinner at someone's house. The way the table was set, the way the food was prepared, and the way the dinner was presented created a marvelous, magical evening. This dinner lasted four hours. It was wonderfully ritualistic. And I kept thinking that the whole ritual of this dinner was a kind of beautiful prayer. One of my favorite icons—Christian artwork designed to create a sense of prayer—pictures the Father, Son, and Holy Spirit sitting down at a table together and going through the ritual of breaking bread. It is a way of praying. And that night in the midst of all the dinner rituals and friendship sharing I experienced prayer.

For those of you with young children, tucking your children into bed at night is a kind of ritual. I hope you say prayers with them, but that act of tucking them in and communicating your love for them before they go to sleep is an unspoken prayer. It's a ritual, but the ritual is a prayer. We might be surprised as parents how that ritual will shape that's child's orientation toward God.

I know Vietnam veterans who have made their way to the Vietnam Memorial in Washington, D.C. While they stand before that wall and read the names in silence, many times they are speechless. They don't have to say a word. They don't have to explain what they think. They don't have to be articulate at that moment about what they are feeling. The ritual of simply going to the wall, of reading the names, of touching the stone, of remembering becomes a prayer. Even their tears become prayers.

A friend of mine took a two-week vacation last fall and visited all the places where he had lived as a boy and where he and his wife had lived when they were first married. He went back to those spots, saw some of the people from his past, and ate at some of the same restaurants in which he used to eat. His whole vacation became a kind of holy pilgrimage. It was a ritual trip, but the ritual became a kind of prayer of thanksgiving for his past, empowering him to move on into his future.

All rituals—going to a class reunion, attending a retirement party, framing a special photograph, having a portrait painted, buying a blue blouse that catches your soulful glance—become connectors with the sacred energy of God. The ordinary becomes extraordinary! These are the rituals that become our wordless prayers.

There's one more mental picture of praying that I would suggest. It is *praying as artistic contemplation.* I love the arts. The arts entertain, to be sure. But I especially love the arts because they have the power to create a sense of depth within us. That's what the spiritual life is all about; it's about depth. I don't know when it happened, but for many of us we got the idea that being "spiritual" means doing lots of "good things" or "church things." Given the fact that many in our culture are on the verge of exhaustion with the stress of children and families and jobs, doing more doesn't seem to be much good news for our already overdone lives. We need to do good things and church things. As a minister in a congregation I'm grateful for all the many activities my members do, but the point of spirituality is to increase a depth of soul and to create a depth of spirit. What's sobering is that we can do all kinds of busy activities, even good ones, and still be spiritually empty.

And so one way to pray is to take time to contemplate art. I would define art broadly. For example, when was the last time you soulfully listened to music? I don't mean the last time you had the radio blaring in the car. But when was the last time you heard music, really heard it? Listen to Bach's *Arioso* or *Air.* Listen. Listen to the patterns of jazz in Dave Brubeck's "Take Five" or "Tangerine." Listen. Listen to the spiritual energy of Mahalia Jackson or the mystery of Van Morrison. Listen. Listen. I write today plugged into the pop/jazz/blues singer Sting. My listening becomes a way of praying. Yesterday I listened to Kathleen Battle sing the poetry of Toni Morrison. Extraordinary. Take time in the quiet of your home, and listen to music. What can happen is that—with or without words—music can become a prayer. The composition of music can help us as we compose a praying life.

Henry Nouwen wrote an entire book about his spiritual experience with a single painting he contemplated one afternoon in an European art museum. He gazed upon Rembrandt's *The Return of the Prodigal Son* until the painting became a prayer inside him. Isn't that remarkable? One painting changed his life forever.

I admire the photography of Edward Weston. His photography moves me, touches me. When I contemplate it, I walk away with an increased capacity of depth. Some of his photographs have become for me prayers. Recently I was given a photograph by Jeffrey Becom. To this day it is the best gift I have ever received in my entire life. The images this up-and-coming photographer offers are nothing less than stunning. To see his Cibachrome images is to see into the heart and soul of God.

There's another dimension to praying and art, and it is the experience of telling stories. How often we have silence in our lives. Not silence as creative solitude, but the shutdown silence of not telling, not talking, not sharing. In many families the message communicated has been, "Keep quiet. We don't talk about those things."

Yet, human beings crave stories the way the way wolves crave food. We need the stories of parents and grandparents. We need the stories of other generations. In these stories we find continuity with our past and healing for our future. Some of the stories we need will bring us pain, but pain is often the beginning point of renewal. Some of the stories will make us laugh. How holy and healing laughter can become for us.

Several years ago, when my children were young, I took them to Cape Cod for a vacation. For a week I rented a place called the Barnstead. Well, that's what it was; it was a barn, and as far as barns go, it was fixed up nicely. I thought it was delightfully rustic, but my kids have teased me relentlessly through the years about the vacation in the barn, no television, and later I was to learn, "That place had lots of spider webs, Dad!"

Yet, not long ago at dinner we were talking about vacations and one of the children started telling the story of the Barnstead again. How many times I had heard it before! But after my ritual teasing one of them asked, "Do you think we could go back there someday?" Wonderful! This story has taken its place in our permanent collection of family stories and holds us together, holds even the presence of God for us. The telling of stories can become an artistic way of praying.

For some it may be a special movie. For others it might be poetry. For some it might be novels or short stories. Music. Photography. Dance. Opera. Classical music. Folk music. Jazz music. Gardening is artistic. One of the legacies of the state of Kentucky is the simple beauty of Shaker furniture. It's functional, of course, but in it beauty and function become one. Telling stories. Opening our eyes and ears to art can dig the reservoir of God's Spirit inside us even deeper. The contemplation of art can indeed become some of our most meaningful prayers. The poet Stanly Kunitz has said it beautifully, "Art is the chalice into which we pour transcendence."

The psalm for our reflection was not said as a traditional prayer with a psalmist kneeling down at his bedside, hands folded, saying a few words to God. Instead, this psalm offers a different mental picture. This psalm was actually a marching psalm. A prayer of ascent. The Jewish people would pray this psalm while marching in a group toward Jerusalem in order to worship God. Probably they were singing it as they marched the dusty roads of the Middle East. This experience of prayer engaged their bodies, filled their hearts, moved them down the road. It's not how we conventionally pray today, but prayer isn't always conventional.

A recent Gallup Poll indicated that 90 percent of all Americans pray and that 75 percent of all Americans pray every single day. There are many ways to pray, and I would encourage you to look for ways to expand your own prayer life. Prayer as conversation. Prayer as reading. Prayer as ritual. Prayer as artistic contemplation.

Ask. Seek. Knock. The essence of prayer is not the words you say, but the soul connection you make. When you do make that divine connection, it changes you forever. Prayer can happen at any moment, in a variety of ways, under any circumstance. Marching to Jerusalem can be a prayer, but so can a ride on a New York City subway or a commuter flight to Chicago for a business meeting. Reading the Bible can become a way of praying, but so can reading the newspaper. It could be a painting hanging in an art museum. A play. A movie. It could be the simple ritual of daily shaving or closing your eyes to go to sleep at night. Ask. Seek. Knock.

QUESTIONS FOR REFLECTION AND DISCUSSION

1. What is your primary mental picture of praying?
2. Have you ever prayed and afterward had better clarity or insight about what you should do next? Describe that time.
3. Try reading a passage of scripture and using a line to repeat as a prayer over and over again. How does that feel to you? Is it a meaningful way of praying?
4. What stories do you tell in your families that become like prayers?
5. Have you ever been moved by a work of art? If so, describe those feelings. How is being moved by art a way of praying?

III

JESUS

7
WHO
WAS
JESUS?

After this he went out and saw a tax collector named Levi,
sitting at the tax booth; and he said to him, "Follow me."
And he got up, left everything, and followed him.

Then Levi gave a great banquet for him in his house; and
there was a large crowd of tax collectors and others sitting
at the table with them. The Pharisees and their scribes
were complaining to his disciples, saying, "Why do you eat
and drink with tax collectors and sinners?" Jesus answered,
"Those who are well have no need of a physician, but those
who are sick; I have come to call not the righteous but
sinners to repentance."

Luke 5:27–32

When I was a boy there was a game show on television titled
To Tell the Truth. The show's format featured a celebrity panel of
questioners and three guests, who would say, one right after the
other, "*My* name is Jane Doe," "*My* name is Jane Doe," and finally, "*My* name is Jane Doe."

The job of the panelists was to ask the right questions in
order to figure out which person was actually Jane Doe and which
were the impostors. After the questioning period, the panelists
would write down their best guesses as to who the real Jane Doe

was. The game would end with the announcer dramatically saying, "Will the *real* Jane Doe please stand up?" And sure enough,
one of the guests would stand, and the panelists either would be
right or surprisingly stumped.

I think many of us have asked a similar question of our faith—
Will the real Jesus please stand up?

Who was Jesus? What kind of person was he? What did he
do? What did he teach? For what did he stand? What did he know
about himself? What was his relationship with God? What was
Jesus all about?

I know those questions may seem simple, especially if you
have gone to church most of your life. But the truth is that the
answers to these questions are immensely complicated. Not complicated in an overwhelming or discouraging way, but, like a good
recipe—with lots of good ingredients that are challenging to put
together—the end presentation is delicious and well worth the
wait.

In this chapter I want to help you understand why it is *so
complex* to know something about this person named Jesus who
walked and lived in Palestine nearly two thousand years ago. Don't
get discouraged by this complexity, but stay with it step by step as
we see an unfolding process and picture of Jesus. Additionally,
after looking at the complexity of the process of learning about
Jesus, I want to make some practical suggestions about who Jesus
was and what his life was about. These suggestions will have far-
reaching implications about how we try to live our Christian lives
today.

How do we know what we know about Jesus? When you open
the part of the Bible we call the New Testament, you first see four
books called "the Gospels." Matthew, Mark, Luke, and John give
us the most information about this person who is commonly called
Jesus of Nazareth. When you read these books, it more or less
appears that they are telling the biographical story of Jesus. The
stories feel much like journalistic accounts of what Jesus said and
did. This is why the Gospels occasionally are called "accounts" of
the life of Jesus. The Gospels include certain highlights such as
Jesus' birth, experiences with his followers, stories and teachings,
and his last week on this earth, including incidents such as the

Last Supper with the disciples, his crucifixion, and the reporting of his resurrection.

When I first started reading the Bible, I assumed that I could take these four accounts of the life of Jesus, put them together in some sort of coherent fashion, and have a fairly accurate picture of the life of Jesus. And I daresay that most of us read the Gospels this way or were given the impression in Sunday school that we could read the Gospels in this way. In my mind, the Four Gospels became one story.

A parable from Luke's Gospel, for example, was much like a parable from Matthew's Gospel, and to quote John's Gospel was similar to quoting from a passage in Mark's Gospel. I just assumed they were all saying the same thing. I remember hearing ministers preach from Luke's Gospel and then in the same sermon preach from John's Gospel or Matthew's Gospel or Mark's Gospel. They gave the impression that there was really only one story of Jesus. The Four Gospels were blended together like different vegetables in a juicer, and all distinction of flavors was lost.

I want to suggest that there is a better way of reading the Gospels, learning about the life of Jesus, and making application of his life story to our lives today. In many ways, it is just as important to know *how* the Gospels were written as it is to understand *what* actually is written in them.

The starting point is *context*. In the first-century world of Palestine there was a social context. We have social context in our country today. The latest MTV video is context. Beautiful suburbs and declining inner cities are part of a social context. Computers are part of a context. Television. Radio. CD players. Buses. Cars. All of these are part of our context, part of our social and cultural world.

In the first century, especially related to Jesus, was a context of Judaism. Generally speaking, Judaism existed as a minority group in a Roman culture. Judaism was a religious countermovement, if you will, on the sidelines from the main sources of social and political power wielded by Rome. Additionally, there were different types of Judaism. Just as we have different Christian denominations, there were different "brands" or "styles" of Judaism. Sometimes in the Gospels these are lumped together as if there were just one Judaism, but in the historical setting of the world of Jesus there were distinctive types of Judaism. Sometimes these different forms of Judaism shared ideas in common, and sometimes they conflicted with bitter intensity.

It is important to understand that Jesus was living in that Roman world and was part of that context, as well as the more immediate context of his Jewish heritage. Yes, Jesus was a Jew. Never once did he deny his Jewish context, and—from all that can be gathered through scholarly research—he did not come to start a new religion that would replace Judaism. Jesus saw himself as a practicing, faithful Jew, and never once did he waver from the faith of his context. This is important to remember and understand because for too long Christians have expressed negative attitudes and actions toward the Jewish faith when, in fact, there would be no Christian faith without the context of the Judaism of Jesus— the context in which Jesus lived and revealed the radical love of God.

Thus into this first-century *context* was born and lived a *person* simply called Jesus of Nazareth. There is not one serious critic who doubts the historical reality of this person. Yet his historical life raises contemporary questions. What was this person Jesus like? What was his essential nature?

Piecing together the various pictures of his life, it appears he was born of poor parents and practiced the Jewish faith from childhood. He grew to be a charismatic religious leader, taking his place alongside rabbis and other religious leaders. There is no indication that he had formal, professional religious training, but he gained popularity with people through his insights into faith, his remarkable wisdom about people, his telling of stories, his use of memorable sayings, and his compelling religious energy. A following grew around him. It would be safe to say that most of his followers were Jewish, though there are indications that he had a wider audience. Jesus was not teaching a new faith; he was bringing new insight into an old one.

A certain kind of ironic picture developed around Jesus. On the one hand, he was a simple Jewish peasant. On the other hand, his religious insight became so compelling and his following so large that Roman officials began seeing him as a threat to the well-being of the state. He threatened the power structures of his day. Roman leaders became scared that Jesus was going to hurt national security. Perhaps the sheer size of crowds following Jesus scared the Romans. Maybe it was the kind of people Jesus was attracting—the poor, the malcontents, the dangerous criminals, the prostitutes—all social undesirables. Maybe it was because Jesus preached a message of justice and social reform that brought fundamental challenges to the Roman leaders.

Regardless of the reason, the Roman government perceived Jesus as a national threat and made the decision to get rid of him. The Romans eliminated Jesus in the same way they had eliminated criminals through the years; they crucified him. Strictly from the perspective of history, the Jews never practiced crucifixion. Certainly it is possible that there were Jewish enemies of Jesus. But if this were so, that number would have been small, with the weight of the responsibility of the crucifixion resting on Roman soldiers and politicians.

However, if you have ever had a plan backfire on you, then you know something of what happened to the Romans. Yes, they did kill Jesus. But instead of Jesus' disciples disappearing into the cultural woodwork, they reported that he had come back to life and that his message and personal presence were still living with them. And although I address the meaning of resurrection in chapter 9, what can be said at this point is that a remarkably alive and vibrant religious intensity gathered around the experience of the risen Christ.

Death was not a period, but a comma. A religious movement was born. A fire that once had been a spark now had become a blaze. The love and hope embodied in this Jewish peasant had proved more powerful than the hate and violence of the Roman government. The Jesus followers were back in business, only now with stronger and renewed convictions.

These "Jesus people" became an identifiable group in the first-century world, and they sometimes were called the *church*. The word *church* literally means "a people called out for a special purpose." In the early years of the church these people remained practicing Jews. That may surprise those of us who are Christians today. But in the early years of the Christian faith, Jesus' disciples remained Jewish-Christians, or Jews who found compelling truth in the life story of Jesus. For them, Jesus was not a founder of a new religion, but a rabbi (religious teacher) who helped them understand God in a new and transformative way. They continued worshiping in the temple and went to their synagogues. But they did something else.

These early followers of Jesus kept his message alive through the retelling of his life stories, his teachings, his parables, and the events of his death and resurrection. What they told became a body of *verbally told Jesus material*. Thus, we move from Jewish-Roman context and the life of Jesus to the retelling of this oral material about Jesus. They kept this body of material alive because they wanted to teach new Christians about Jesus. They wanted to teach their children about Jesus. When they had their gatherings or services they would preach sermons, and they needed material to use to help people deepen their understanding of Jesus. They frequently would have a ceremony using bread and wine—later called communion or eucharist—in which they would give thanks for Jesus' life; they would use this Jesus material during the ceremony.

It just makes sense, doesn't it? Because the followers of Jesus wanted to keep recollections about him fresh and alive, they passed on verbally stories to one another. Remember, there were no printing presses and really no inclination to write down all of this material because Jesus' followers expected him to return at any time. For the earliest Christians, telling the oral stories was enough. And what should not be overlooked is that they retold the Jesus stories, not to preserve history as we think of history today, but to reach into people's lives for the purpose of spiritual transformation.

Yet, as the generations grew older, they began to realize a new step needed to be taken. They wanted more than just verbal stories; they wanted written stories about Jesus. And that's exactly what started to happen thirty to forty years after his life on earth. People began *writing and collecting written Jesus material*. In all likelihood, these were collections of parables or written collections of teachings organized in a way that could be used for instructing new members of the church community.

Notice the progression so far:
1. *The social **context** of a Roman world and Jewish culture.*
2. *The presence of a historical **person** called Jesus of Nazareth.*
3. *The community of dedicated followers called the **church**.*
4. *The preservation of Jesus through the retelling of **verbal stories**.*
5. *The transformation of verbal stories into **written collections** used in the church.*

It is as important to understand the *process* of how we learn about Jesus as it is to understand the final *product* of Jesus himself. What we know of Jesus today is part of an unfolding process, and that process, rather than detracting from our appreciation and love of Jesus, actually enhances our relationship with him.

The last stage of this process is actually *the writing of this innovative, artistic, communication form called a gospel.* Most New Testament scholars now agree that the Gospel of Mark was the first Gospel written. It was written, not to give a biography of Jesus, but to tell a congregation about the good news of Jesus and to give them insight into how to live their life of faith. Mark, no doubt, incorporated into his writings some of the verbal stories he had heard. He used some of the written collections that circulated in the churches too. But it was Mark who boldly had the idea to weave together the stories and sayings of Jesus into one coherent, beginning-to-end, start-to-finish presentation of Jesus.

After Mark wrote his Gospel, others followed suit and wrote their presentations. Matthew, who like Mark was a minister to a church, wrote his Gospel. However, Matthew not only was able to use verbal and written materials that circulated about Jesus, but he also had the added luxury of using Mark's Gospel as a source for his writing project. This is why sometimes Matthew tells a story exactly the same way that Mark does in his Gospel and at other times tells the story in a slightly or drastically different way. Luke did the same in his writing process. John's Gospel, which is radically different from the other three, appears to be a much more independent writing project and written significantly later than the other three. The first three Gospels—Matthew, Mark, and Luke—are called the *Synoptic Gospels* because they can be "seen together" in such an interrelated way.

It is important to remember that all the Gospel writers were writing their works, not to make photocopies of all the historical words and actions of Jesus, but to tell the story of Jesus in a way that would help strengthen the faith of Jesus' followers. These writers told the Jesus story from their own perspectives. Each of these evangelists was trying to share the essential life of Jesus with his respective congregation. They addressed specific needs in their congregations. They were not historians. They were not biographers. They were not stenographers. They were not journalists. They were preachers proclaiming that the presence of God had drawn near to the world in a decisive and compelling way through the person of Jesus of Nazareth. They were trying to express their message through the literary form of the gospel document.

I'm aware that to hear that the Gospels "developed" through various stages, as opposed to being "given" to us by God in complete and final form, is disturbing for some people. Once during a workshop I led on the formation of the Bible, a woman raised her hand and asked, "Don't you believe in the inspiration of the Bible?" I could feel her anxiety and worry. I explained that if by inspiration she meant that God dictated exact words into the minds of Matthew, Mark, Luke, and John, who then wrote down those words—with each word's being 100 percent historically accurate and without any connection to first-century culture—then I didn't believe in *that kind* of inspiration.

I went on to say that if by inspiration she meant that God was involved in the historical process of the stages and that when we read the Gospels today we can discover the living word of God for our lives—a word that is authoritative and transformative for the church—then I do believe in *that way* of understanding inspiration. Inspiration simply means that the breath or Spirit of God is alive and present in the documents. I believe this to be so. Yet, this breath is present, not by delivering a finished package of writings to the earth, but by what the words can do when people of faith read them and listen to them.

In many ways the Gospel writers did what your minister tries to do every Sunday from the pulpit. When I preach a sermon, I'm trying to connect the good news of God with specific needs in my congregation. I don't use mail-order sermons. I don't preach sermons that someone else has written. To do that would be to ignore the context of my church, not to mention the authentic experiences of my own life. I listen to the joy and pain of my church members and then try to speak a word from God that makes a difference in their lives.

In the same way, when you look at the Four Gospels you see four distinct portraits of Jesus. They have some degree of historical accuracy. But more than being historical photographs, they are theological portraits painted many years after the life of Jesus.

If that is how the Gospel documents came into being, the question still remains, *"So, what was Jesus really like?"* Our reflection text has some interesting insights into the life of Jesus. Remember, we are looking at Luke's portrait of Jesus. Nevertheless, inside the portrait are indications of what Jesus was like in his earthly life.

On the surface, the story seems innocent enough. Jesus sees a man by the name of Levi who is a tax collector. Jesus invites him to the adventure of discipleship, and Levi accepts. That is the nature of discipleship. We feel this call to attend to our spiritual lives, and then we follow it. This call to follow, to attend to the needs of our soul, comes to us in subtle and mysterious ways. Joseph Campbell called it "following your bliss." Regardless of the language, discipleship is about following the spiritual promptings and inklings that come our way.

Several years ago we had some friends who lived in Michigan. As children, our friends had gone to church, but when they left home, they stopped attending church. They married, but still never attended church. They had children, but never connected with a faith community. When their kids were small, their first grader saw a book in a bookcase. It was a book her mother had received when she was baptized as a young girl.

The little girl said, "Mommy, what's this book?"

Her mother, embarrassed, said, "That's a Bible, honey."

That night the mother said to her husband, "You can go or you can stay. But the kids and I are going to church Sunday, and we're going to find a church home. We owe it to the kids." And they did. They worship every Sunday now at a Presbyterian church. Their lives changed when they finally listened to the prompting.

Dan Wakefield opens his moving spiritual autobiography *Returning* with these words: "One balmy spring morning in Hollywood, a month or so before my forty-eighth birthday, I woke up screaming. I got out of bed, went into the next room, sat down on a couch, and screamed again . . . it was a response to the reality that another morning had broken in a life I could only deal with sedated by wine, loud noise, moving images, and wired to electronic games . . . the day I woke up screaming I grabbed from among my books an old Bible I hadn't opened for nearly a quarter of a century. With a desperate instinct I turned to the Twenty-third Psalm and read it over, several times. . . ."

A few months later Dan Wakefield would venture out alone, walk down a street as a solitary figure, and go to a Christmas Eve church service. He would write of that church, "I looked inside and saw a beginning." How's that for a prompting?

What Jesus did with Levi and what he does again and again in our lives is to invite, open the door, point the way. Sometimes there is the faint whisper that something is missing in our lives, and that becomes a call to follow. Occasionally the anguish of a dark night of the soul is the call we need to begin the spiritual journey. Maybe it is the experience of sheer joy in life that finally opens the door to give thanks to the one who is the Creator of all life's joy. Whatever the promptings, they can become the soulful invitations of Jesus to become followers. Levi was called and followed. We must do the same.

What's remarkable about this calling of Levi is that he was a *tax collector*. That may not seem like much to us. Most tax collectors and CPAs in our society are well respected and exist in the mainstream of society. But remember, this story has a first-century context. In the time of Jesus, the social world was divided quite sharply between the religiously *accepted* and *unaccepted*, the religious *insiders* and *outsiders*. The social boundaries between those two groups were sharp and firm.

Who was the insider? During the time of Jesus, the religious insider was the person who followed a strict purification system of religion. I cannot exaggerate how complex this system of rules and regulations had become. If a person remained religiously pure—ate only pure foods, did all the right ceremonial washing, and maintained a household that followed all the religious purification laws—then that person was considered clean and acceptable, a religious insider.

This is why certain people were upset when Jesus gleaned food on the Sabbath. An insider would not do that because to gather or prepare food on the Sabbath was to break a ceremonial law. When Jesus healed people the religious insiders often were offended because Jesus would touch the ill person, and to touch a person with a disease automatically made you an unclean person. A wounded person was unclean. A woman having her period was unclean. A person maimed in an accident was unclean. The purity system demanded perfection, and this invariably led to people feeling one of two ways—either spiritually crushed over their failure to live up to the demands of the system or self-righteous to the point that they thought they were better than everyone else.

Who was the outsider? The outsider was the person who did not follow the purification system. Notice that an outsider could have been what we might perceive as a good person, even a religious person, but because he or she did not follow the purification system—or even lapsed and violated the system—that person was considered an outsider and completely unacceptable to the religious community. There was no margin for error. You were either in or out. Good or bad. Righteous or unrighteous. The distinctions were sharp and severe.

The tax collectors were outsiders because they worked for the Roman government and failed to follow the purity system. When Luke writes about Jesus' calling "sinners," he does not mean that Jesus was calling all the people who had done something wrong at one time or another in their lives. "Sinner," at least in Luke's Gospel, means someone who was unacceptable, outside the religious purity system, a person on the margins of society. Imagine the pain of this situation. If you were an outsider, you lived with little hope of God, no sense of community, and no religious identity to nurture your life.

It is in this social context that Jesus lived. Do you want to know what Jesus was about? Jesus was about turning this socially divided world upside-down and inside-out, setting it on its head. Jesus was about bringing God to the very people who thought

God was out of reach and reaching people who had been told in various ways that they were unacceptable to God.

And that's exactly what you see in this reflection text. Not only does Levi respond to the invitation of Jesus to become a disciple, but he takes Jesus home with him and invites all his tax-collecting buddies over for dinner. They have one big raucous party, and Jesus eats with them. What a controversy! What a religious travesty! Those in the purity system who were watching from the sidelines shook their heads and said, "How can he call himself a religious leader, spiritual, a man of God, and still associate with those *sinners*?" I can just see them with their binoculars, watching Jesus from a distance.

You have to give them credit. The self-righteous critics who were standing on the sidelines and doing their religious surveillance understood exactly what was going on. In the world of Jesus, to eat with someone was to endorse that person, accept him or her, and extend friendship. You don't eat with just anybody. Sharing table fellowship meant to be in relationship with the other person eating bread and drinking wine across the table. The fact that Jesus would eat with sinners was his way of saying, "You are not an outsider to God. You are accepted by God. You are loved by God. You are friends with God, and God is friend to you." Wow! No wonder they were having a party! And no wonder this book is a good news book!

In fact, in Luke 4, when Jesus preaches his first sermon, he is quite clear. He declares: "I have come to bring good news to the poor." It was good news because, in the world of Jesus, the rich were thought to have been blessed by God. (After all, they got their blessings from God, didn't they?) And as for the poor, they were totally unacceptable because they had not been blessed by God and were therefore distanced from God. (Unfortunately, our culture sometimes gives the impression that the poor are poor because they deserve it.) But not according to Jesus.

"I have come to proclaim release to the captives. . . ." The captives were obviously (at least to the religious insiders) people who had done wrong things. (Why else would they be in prison?) Therefore, they were unacceptable to the religious community. But not in the eyes of Jesus.

"I have come to bring recovery of sight to the blind. . . ." The blind, like all people with disease, were thought to have their "disease" as a sign of God's punishment. If they were being punished by God, then they were totally unacceptable to the religious community. But not from the perspective of Jesus.

Over and over again Jesus exploded social boundaries by loving the unlovable, accepting the unacceptable, and affirming the rejected. This is why Jesus created such angry critics. His way of relating was based on love and compassion, whereas others had a religion based on correctness and rightness. Jesus always was more concerned about being alive than about being right.

This essence of Jesus is crucial to our lives in many ways, and I want to suggest some implications for us:

1. This essence of Jesus is crucial to each of us personally because there is a part of all of us that feels unacceptable to God. In his relationship with persons, Jesus does not start with what is wrong with them (or us) but with what *is* acceptable. We may do bad things, but that does not mean we are bad people. And even when we do bad things, God does not stop loving us. We were not created to wallow before God in our mistakes or shortcomings; we were created to be alive and to party, celebrating the presence of God every day! Wouldn't it make a difference if your approach to God was love and celebration instead of attempts to be more and better? A man said to me, "I wouldn't live the Christian life if it weren't for fear of going to hell when I die." I thought to myself, "How sad! How sad that his whole orientation toward God is to avoid being punished." The God of Jesus is not a God of fear and punishment, but of love and celebration. What if Jesus cares more about your being alive than he does about your being better? Believe me, that's exactly what happened at that little impromptu tax collectors' convention two thousand years ago—love brought people back to life!

2. This essence of Jesus is helpful in defining the mission of the church. If you go to church regularly, think about this—Who are the most important people to your church community? Where is most of the church's focus? Where does most of the money go? What takes most of your minister's time? My guess is that in most churches the focus is on our own members. Insiders! What if this

Jesus essence turned our churches upside-down and inside-out and
we started to take seriously what we need to do to reach those
outside the church, those who never felt comfortable in a church
before, those for whom church always has been something someone else does? What if that meant that we had to change our music? Change the way we preach sermons? Change the way we dress
for church? What would happen if we started to make the needs
and hurts and sorrows of nonmembers more a focus for the church
than the feelings and quirks and complaints of our own members?
What if you led your church to love one group of unacceptable
people in our society? AIDS patients. Cancer patients. Children.
Teenagers. Elderly people. Mentally ill people. Homeless people.
Refugees.

After the tax collectors' banquet the critics of Jesus ask him
point-blank: "Why do you eat with tax collectors and sinners?"

Jesus responds with forthrightness and clarity: "Those who
are well have no need of a physician, but those who are sick; I have
come to call not the righteous but sinners to repentance." Ahh,
that's it!

The "righteous" were those in the inside circle of the purification system; the "sinners" were all those on the outside. To call
people to repentance means to call people to live with a *new brain.*
That's literally what the word *repentance* means—"to have a new
mind," a new way of thinking and seeing and looking at the world.
Repentance is not so much remorse for doing bad things as it is
discovering joy in seeing new ways. Repentance is a call to adventure. That's what this historical figure Jesus was all about, helping
people see and feel and come alive. His message was simple good
news.

Will the real Jesus please stand up?

I think the real Jesus did stand up that day when he ate dinner with the sinners. He does today too—every time he comes
home with us, accepting that in us which we won't even accept
ourselves, and every time we extend that acceptance and compassion to another human being, he comes home with us. He comes
home with me and you and the stranger on the outskirts of our
mind and says, "You are my friend! Let's have a party!"

QUESTIONS FOR REFLECTION AND DISCUSSION

1. Imagine you are talking to a person who literally has never heard of Jesus of Nazareth. How would you describe this historical figure?
2. What about Jesus do you most like? What about Jesus most disturbs you?
3. Are the Gospel documents strict journalistic accounts of Jesus or more like theological portraits? Why does it matter?
4. The fact that the Gospels developed is sometimes a new concept. Why is it important to understand how the Gospels came to be?
5. Who are the "insiders" and "outsiders" of our world today? What are the implications for the church today?

8

What Is the
MEANING
of the Symbol of
THE CROSS?

*For the message about the cross is foolishness to those who
are perishing, but to us who are being saved it is the power
of God. For it is written, "I will destroy the wisdom of the
wise, and the discernment of the discerning I will thwart."*

*Where is the one who is wise? Where is the scribe? Where is
the debater of this age? Has not God made foolish the wisdom of the world? For since, in the wisdom of God, the
world did not know God through wisdom, God decided,
through the foolishness of our proclamation, to save those
who believe. For Jews demand signs and Greeks desire wisdom, but we proclaim Christ crucified, a stumbling block
to Jews and foolishness to Gentiles, but to those who are the
called, both Jews and Greeks, Christ the power of God and
the wisdom of God. For God's foolishness is wiser than
human wisdom, and God's weakness is stronger than human strength.*

1 Corinthians 1:18–25

A few months ago on a narrow country road near my house
there was a tragic automobile accident. I didn't personally know
anyone involved, but I read about it in the newspaper. Three teen-

agers were in the car. Two were seriously injured. The other teenager died instantly.

Evidently, when they came upon a sharp curve the car went straight and hit an old sycamore tree head-on. The whole community was in shock because the teenager who died was extremely popular and an excellent student at the local high school. Since that accident, every time I drive on that road and pass that tree, I think of that teenager and the sadness of her life coming to such a premature end.

To make the point even more vividly, each time I drive past that tree I see symbols. Blue and white cheerleader pom-poms have been placed there by friends because she had been on the high-school cheerleading squad. Wilted daisies and scraggly black-eyed susans are lying on the ground beside the tree too—signs of a dear friend missed by other classmates who occasionally come by and place flowers at the tree. And propped up against the exposed bark of the tree is a handmade wooden cross, painted white with a purple ribbon that reads: "We miss you."

Symbols are powerful, aren't they? Some people think of symbols as decorations. Mere representations of the real thing. Ornamentation. This is expressed when someone says, "Oh, that's *just* a symbol." It's as if the person is saying that because something is a symbol it's not all that important, it's not quite real, it's not to be taken too seriously. Icing on the cake perhaps, but not as important as the real thing, the real feeling, or the real idea. Just a symbol.

Symbols. What do symbols do? What does it mean to say something is symbolic? What is the power of symbols?

Symbols are key to understanding the Christian faith. That especially is true in trying to understand the meaning of the death and resurrection of Jesus Christ. The cross is a symbol—not a *mere* symbol, not *just* a symbol, not *simply* a symbol, but a symbol that has a depth of spiritual and psychological meaning for the person who is ready to see it.

Frequently I notice that when people become interested in the Bible for the first time, they begin to literalize what the Bible says, not just the literalization of a particular text, but the whole story of Jesus is understood at a wooden, literal level. They tend to

focus on the surface details or become concerned with the historical telling of the biblical story. What they miss is the symbolic
nature of what is being portrayed. Symbols have depth. Symbols
live inside the human soul. We might not be able to explain what
they mean at a conscious level, but they are inside us and move us.
Unless religious symbols like the cross are appreciated at a soul
level, the Christian faith is never genuinely understood, or at least
it is not understood at a level of depth.

When I drive past that sycamore tree and see the pom-poms
or the flowers or that cross leaning against the tree, I know that I
am seeing a whole world of meaning. Those symbols mean something. I might not be able to explain the depth of their meaning.
In fact, I'm sure I can't know what those other classmates are feeling as they mourn the loss of their friend. But I can at least approach some of their world and participate in some of their life
because of the power of those symbols. The symbols invite my
participation into a world of feeling and meaning and human experience, and not just the classmates' feelings. As I drive past that
tree, I am surprisingly in touch with my own feelings and thoughts.
Even my own sense of mortality rises up inside me, and I wonder
about the meaning of my own life—who I am and what I am
about. Symbols do that. They aren't decorations for a tree; they
become invitations to know ourselves better.

Sure I could say, "Well, those are *just* flowers." Or "Those are
just blue and white strings of plastic attached to the end of a stick."
Or "Those are *just* two pieces of wood nailed together—one running vertically, the other placed horizontally—propped up against
an old sycamore tree." But if that were my approach, then I would
be flattening out all the complexity and meaning of the symbols,
muting their power to speak to my soul, and sadly cutting off the
depth of life flow they could create inside me. When we flatten
out symbols, it's like drinking a soft drink that's been sitting out
for two days—all the fizz is gone! Symbols want to fizz, to be
effervescent, they want to bubble up within us.

One night after a performance, someone came backstage and
asked the famed dance teacher and choreographer Martha Gra-
ham, "What did that dance mean?" Her response was perfect. She
said, "If I could have explained it, I wouldn't have had to dance it."

I once was spending an evening with the poet Robert Bly after one of his poetry readings and someone asked him a similar question. "Mr. Bly, would you explain to me the meaning of this poem?" And Robert, known to get a little impatient with questions like that, said in his bombastic way, "If I had wanted to write a damn essay, I would have!" His point was made. Symbols have the power to speak because symbols have something important to say.

What does the symbol of the cross mean?

There are several dimensions of meaning found in the cross. First of all, the cross is a *symbol of the reality of human evil*. In the Roman world the cross was a shock, an embarrassment. The cross was a disturbance and scandal. Criminals were crucified. The fact that Jesus—an innocent man, a man whose primary message was love for all people and acceptance of the unacceptable—was crucified is an indication of the depth of human pain and suffering in this world. For many of us the cross has become too nice, too decorated, and far too pretty. The truth is that in the first-century world crucifixion was scandalous.

Therefore, the cross functions as a symbol that reminds people of just how evil the world can be. No matter how unpleasant that is for us to see or how difficult it is for us to think about, the reality of the cross demands that of us. We do not have to be morbid about the world and walk around depressed about how bad life has become. That kind of resignation does no one any good. What the cross invites us to do is to face squarely the reality of evil in the world. Although the power of evil can be overestimated, it should never be underestimated.

Take a look at what's happening in the world. In 1995 there was an explosion that rocked the soul of this nation when terrorists struck a federal building in Oklahoma City; 168 innocent people, many of them children, were killed. Hundreds more were injured. The photograph of a fireman carrying the body of a baby who had been killed in that explosion was imprinted on the heart of a nation. We could perhaps cope with an earthquake. A hurricane? Well, hurricanes happen. And so do tornadoes and floods. Those kinds of tragedies hurt, but at least they have a place in the larger picture of how the world works. But an event such as the

Oklahoma City bombing is inexplicable. *We* did this to *ourselves*. Such an event catches us off guard. We tend to go about our lives, doing our jobs, making our plans, spending our money. And some of us, not all of us, but some of us are lulled to sleep thinking that the world is a pretty nice place to be. From time to time a few unfortunate things might happen, but all in all the world is a pretty clean and safe and sane place to live.

The cross, however, is a symbol that breaks through to our slumbering complacency and middle-class American optimism and says: "Don't forget, don't underestimate, don't minimize the reality of evil in this world. An innocent man was crucified! Crucified! Don't ever forget it!"

And when you look at the symbol of the cross and that symbol begins doing its breakthrough work, you begin seeing that God—this energy of love and hope in the world—is being crucified over and over again. The bombing in Oklahoma City was a kind of crucifixion. And so is a war that rages in Bosnia. Vietnam was a kind of crucifixion. The rise of domestic violence in our country, which renders the American home more dangerous than it ever has been in the history of this country, is a crucifixion. So is gutted, hopeless, despairing poverty in inner-city neighborhoods. So are environmental deaths to our once lush and life-giving streams and mountains and oceans. Why, we've even managed to crucify the ozone! There are many crucifixions in our world.

The cross is an unforgettable reminder that no matter how well we insulate ourselves and remove ourselves and protect ourselves from life's unpleasant pictures, the pictures are still there. I still have to drive past that old sycamore tree and see that clumsy-looking cross. And, well, I should. Because that cross is a sign that the world does go wrong. In spite of the fact that I want to forget that part of life, the cross won't let me forget. We have human suffering in the world, and the cross demands that we as Christians take that suffering seriously.

"Take up your cross," commanded Jesus. And one way we take up our cross is to be present with the genuine suffering in our own soul, as well as in the lives of others in the world. We can try to entertain ourselves into protective cocoons, which many Americans are trying to do, or spend our way to paradise, which many of us are trying to do with extended family budgets and maxed-out credit cards. We can also try to build walls around our lives to keep out anything undesirable. (Living in gated communities is the trend in housing developments these days.) But the truth of the cross remains—there is evil in the world and in ourselves that cannot be ignored.

In a related way, the cross is a *symbol of the suffering of God.* Yes, we suffer in the rough-and-tumble experiences of this world, and the cross is a breakthrough reminder of that. But God also suffers in this world.

Jesus had come to love deeply three close friends—Mary, Martha, and Lazarus. These were his buddies. For the public he had to be about the business of teaching and preaching. Doing his acts of healing. Responding to the needs of the masses of people that pressed upon him. And even with the disciples Jesus often felt as if he were part referee, part mom, and part high-school principal. But his time with Mary and Martha and Lazarus was different. These were his kick-back-and-relax friends.

One day Jesus was going to visit with them. No doubt he was looking forward to sitting and talking, catching up on their lives, taking it easy. However, on his way to visit he hears that Lazarus is very sick. When Jesus gets there he is greeted by the sisters. They are crying. Sad. Grieving over what has happened and what they must tell Jesus. Grief has many sides. Sometimes there is grief over the actual death; sometimes there is grief over the telling of it.

The way John tells this story in his Gospel is poignant and tender. "Your friend is dead," they say to him. And then in that eleventh chapter of John we have the shortest bit of commentary found in the entire Bible. It reads simply, "Jesus wept." (KJV)

This weeping of Jesus is not mere journalistic reporting; it is an insightful portrait of God. If Jesus wept, then Jesus was touched by the suffering of this world. Not far off. Not cool and aloof. Jesus is on the streets, in the homes, living the human experience. Not a robot dropped down out of the sky by God. Not a celebrity hidden by an entourage of security goons. Not some divine Hercules striding upon the earth immune from the pain and sorrow of human experience. This Jesus is the weeping Jesus, touched by grief to the point of grieving himself.

And what that means for our faith is that this weeping Jesus reveals to us a weeping God. What kind of God is God? Rather than bringing preconceptions about what "God" means, why not start with this picture? Jesus reveals a God who suffers with the pain and hurt of our world—your pain and my pain; the pain of Oklahoma City; and the pain of teenagers at a local high school who mourn the death of a friend.

What kind of God is God? If we let Jesus paint the picture of God, then what we begin to see are the broad, shocking brush strokes of a weeping God who loves the world so much that God suffers over it. Not remote. Not aloof. This God is touched by the world.

Sam is a good friend of mine. He is one of those older men who brings wisdom to my life. We had known each other for a couple of years, but, as is the nature of friendship, there's always more to learn. One day we were talking about children—particularly how what we hope for our children and what our children actually do often clash. We both agreed that as parents we set ourselves up for big-time hurt when we idealize the future of our children too much.

Sam slowly said to me, "You know, I've never told you this before, but I have a son who is thirty-four years old."

"Really. I never knew that," I said.

"Yeah, he lives in Denver."

"Do you see him often?"

"I haven't seen him in a couple of years now."

"Why don't you see him?" I asked.

"Well, you see, he lives on the streets out there."

"What do you mean he lives on the streets?"

"My son," he said with a quivering lip, "my son, you see, is homeless."

Sam went on to explain a long and dramatic story of pain with this young man. How they had tried to get him help. How they had depleted resources trying to help him. How they had been emotionally stretched like a guitar string to the point of breaking so many different times. How his last visit was so destructive that they had to decide the situation was out of their hands and that there was nothing more they could do as parents.

Sam said, "We got to the point two years ago that we decided all we could do was to break all ties with him. But some nights, some nights all I can do is lie in my bed and wonder where he is."

In all my years of ministry I have never heard more parental pain. Where does that suffering come from? I finally have come to believe that suffering and love come from the same place inside our soul. If we did not love, there would be no suffering. We suffer and hurt and weep for our kids late into the night only because we care for them. Sam hurt more deeply than any parent I've been around because he loved as much as any parent I've ever known. We get homesick because we love home so much. We shed tears over someone's death because we loved her living so much. Jesus wept because Jesus loved.

What is revealed in the living and dying of Jesus is a portrait of a God who is the suffering companion with us.

One of the most interesting stories about Jesus is the one of Jesus' losing his temper. I know that many of us as Christians have been taught not to lose our temper, get mad, or lose control of our emotions. Yet that's exactly what happened to Jesus when he entered the temple one day and saw the tables and booths of the money changers. The money changers were part of the religious purity system I talked about in the last chapter. They sold and resold sacrifices, collected taxes from the people to keep the system going, and created a feeling that faith was merely the doing of the ceremony and not the transformation of the heart. This was not true of all Jews, but it was true of some who lived within this highly ritualized religious system.

When Jesus saw this whole scene—a system that created insiders and outsiders, a system of corruption, a system that turned the beauty of worship into a shopping-mall experience—he became angry. Angry! He turned over tables. He glared at the hucksters. He spoke firmly and clearly about keeping the house of God a place of spiritual transformation and worship for all people. But what is insightful here is that Jesus felt so deeply that the injustices and suffering of the world broke through and touched him. And the theological insight that should be remembered is that if Jesus was touched by the events of the world—sometimes sad, sometimes angry—and if he was always present as a suffering friend, then so is God.

What happened in Oklahoma City hurt God. What happened that night on a sharp turn when a car hit a sycamore tree caused God pain and anguish and sorrow. It happens to God every time a life is lost in war or every time a woman is struck with the fist of a man in her own home. God feels it when babies die in explosions and when the elderly are neglected in nursing homes. And as I said earlier, God feels it when church buses crash too. God feels it. Takes it in. Is changed by it. And it happens because God is love.

Dietrich Bonhoeffer was a Christian minister in Germany during World War II. He had a brilliant mind and a bright future. He already had been to America to lecture in some of the country's most prestigious universities. He was a writer with significant promise. The faith of Bonhoeffer, however, caused him to resist Hitler and his Nazi bullies. Bonhoeffer was arrested and put in prison. It has been said that one of Hitler's last orders before his own demise was to have Bonhoeffer executed. Bonhoeffer is truly a modern-day Christian martyr.

Before his death, however, Bonhoeffer wrote several letters in prison. These letters, which were sent to friends and colleagues, have been compiled into a book, *Letters and Papers from Prison*. This book deeply influenced me when I first read it years ago, and I continue to draw inspiration from it. One line in the book is seared upon my brain; to me it represents the symbolic meaning of the cross. Bonhoeffer simply wrote, "Only a suffering God can help."

It is the suffering God whom you see through the cross. You might want to think of God as a satellite dish that picks up television signals. Every moment of suffering, every detail of evil, every second of despair is picked up on the divine satellite dish. God sees it all and feels it all and is affected by it all. Sometimes we want an all-power-filled God. A God who can do anything. A God who can stop car wrecks and prevent bombs from hurting people. A Superman God. But that's not the message of the cross of Jesus. This God is a God who suffers perfectly because this God loves perfectly.

The reflection text is suggestive. "The cross is foolishness," wrote Paul. Scandalous. The cross is not a sign of traditional power; it is a sign of weakness. Isn't that interesting? How many sermons have you heard on the weakness of God? We want God to move mountains. We want God to jump in and rescue. We want God to make it all right. But finally that is not what we really need—and maybe not even what we really want.

This "foolishness" of God's suffering with us is finally "wiser than human wisdom," Paul writes. This "weakness" of God is ultimately "stronger than human strength," Paul proclaims. Therefore, talking about God's being crucified and suffering may sound a little foolish to some who hear us, Paul argues, but to those who are ready to be in relationship with God, this good news message has the power to save them and bring them to wholeness.

The cross is a symbol of human suffering. It is a symbol of divine suffering. And growing from both of those dimensions is a third meaning. The cross is a *symbol of love.*

How much does God love us? The symbol of the cross says that God loves to the point of being crucified at the hands of hateful and vindictive people. You mean that God loves us that much? You mean that God is willing to be crucified by an angry mob even as God invites persons to come and be in a relationship of friendship? That's how much God loves. Just as Sam ached over a homeless son in Denver, so God aches over Sam. If Sam has shed a thousand tears for his son, God has shed a thousand and one. The heartbroken teenagers placing pom-poms and flowers at the foot of a sycamore tree are not alone. God aches and grieves along with them. A bomb may have destroyed a federal building in Oklahoma City, but the way people reached out toward one another, supported and helped one another, the way a whole nation paused and prayed for those people is a sign—a sign that love is stronger than hate, compassion stronger than political fanaticism, and hope deeper than despair. God is here.

The cross reveals that the most enduring power in our lives is God's love. Love becomes the ultimate value that is presented in the cross. Nothing stops God from loving us. Car wrecks can't do it. Neither can car bombs. Getting fired from your job won't do it. Your husband's leaving you after twenty-two years of marriage doesn't diminish God's love either. Your child's becoming a wandering homeless man and breaking your heart and rendering you sleepless night after night won't stop God's love from flowing toward you.

What finally makes life worth living is this precious gift of love that is given to us by God. Some days we feel that love more than other days. At times we feel it and know it, and we are happy. If we would pause and pray and think about being held by divine love, our lives probably would be different from the hurried and frantic pace we often find ourselves in. This is why daily prayer is so important.

So many of us are scrambling from one door to the next, hoping that *this* time we will feel whole. We purchase a new car, but then after awhile that car is just a car. We build a new house and immerse ourselves in the busyness of contractors and wallpaper and color charts. All of that gives our life purpose for a while, but then when that project is over we still are left holding the fragility of our own soul. Some of us find ourselves going round after round with addictions. Addicted to alcohol or drugs or food. And what is an addiction but a desperate cry for spiritual meaning and love? It is love that finally matters. The apostle Paul put it essentially like this in his great chapter on love in 1 Corinthians 13: "If I don't have love, I am nothing!" Indeed, if I don't have God, I am nothing.

The theologian Teilhard de Chardin beautifully captured the central focus of love—not only in the human experience, but in the entire drama of the cosmos—when he wrote: "Someday, after the earth and the waves and the winds are conquered, then man will discover the power of love. And that will be the second time fire is discovered."

Raymond Carver, whom I considered one of the great American writers in my lifetime, died just a few years ago. A relatively young man, Carver battled cancer. In the face of that dreaded disease he sought to discover the meaning of his life during his last months. He wrote this sweet and insightful poem:

> *And did you get what*
> *you wanted from this life, even so?*
> *I did.*

And what did you want?
To call myself beloved, to feel myself
beloved on the earth.

What more do any of us want or need? What else could any
of us ask for? To look at the symbol of the cross is to look at the
best truth of the universe—"I am loved!"

I'm aware that some Christians focus on the cross through
the idea of Jesus' dying for our sins. *What does it mean that Jesus
died for our sins?* Often the presentation goes something like this:
we were all sinners, truly degraded and rotten people. Because God
is so righteous and holy, God has to punish us with death. Death
is not merely the ending of life on earth, but it is separation from
God for eternity, the banishment of all sinners to hell.

Notice that in this line of thinking God is presented as not
wanting to send people to hell, but because God cannot compro-
mise the punishment system, God must send us to hell. Fundamentally, according to this view, God is repulsed by all people
because all people are sinners. In the nick of time, however, God
comes up with a plan: "I'll send my own son, who is sinless and,
therefore, a worthy sacrifice for sin, to die as a substitute for all the
sinners on the earth. He will die so they won't have to die, and his
death will satisfy my need to punish people for their sins. I can
still be loving by giving people an escape route, and I can still be
just by punishing sin." Thus, it is often presented that Jesus died
"in our place," "for our sins," as a "sacrifice on our behalf."

Perhaps you are not familiar with this presentation of the
Christian faith, but my hunch is many of you are. For many years
I thought this was the central truth of the faith and the only way
of understanding the death of Jesus Christ. This particular interpretation no longer makes sense to me, and I no longer hold it to
be true.

There are so many problems with this presentation. First of
all, the presentation begins with God's being angry and ready to
punish wicked sinners, such as you and me. My understanding of
God is that God is love and looks at our brokenness as something
to heal, not something to punish. Second, this presentation de-
picts a God who must have a human sacrifice in order to satisfy
the need to punish. If a parent did that we would think him or her

reprehensible. Why should God be exempt from the standards of decency we hold to be true? Third, it seems that this whole way of thinking is a fantasy make-believe game. To think that someone can be punished for us or serve a sentence on our behalf doesn't make sense. It sounds like a religious word game. How, after all, could Jesus be punished for what I have done? If God wanted to punish me in the first place—I don't think God wants to, but for the sake of argument—how could Jesus take a punishment that I deserve? It doesn't make sense. Fourth, this scheme of salvation does not take into account the healing the entire world needs from sin. It's not just people who need the love of God, but the oceans and mountains and entire scarred and wounded universe. In this sense, all the world suffers from sin—that is, brokenness—and needs God's love and healing.

In case you are wondering, the previous presentation of the Christian faith is called the doctrine of *substitutionary atonement*. It is certainly more complicated than I've presented here, but I think you can get some idea of the reasoning behind it. Although there are some hints of it at certain places in the Bible, there is never a full-blown doctrine of it. This doctrine became more developed by the theologian Anselm several centuries ago.

For me today to say that "Jesus died for my sins" means that *Jesus lived and revealed a God of unconditional love and it is love that heals my brokenness as a person.* That's the good news of the Christian faith, and that is my salvation.

What does the symbol of the cross mean? The cross is a sign of human suffering in the world. The cross is a sign of God's suffering in the world. The cross is a sign of love—unconditional love that endures with us through our little deaths each day, our final death when we pass from this world to the next, and even beyond death.

Beyond death? How can love endure beyond death? What might that mean for us? How can the grand ending of the story of Jesus become a beginning for you and me? New beginnings! That's resurrection. And that is why the story of the cross and the resurrection must always be told together. It's to a new beginning we turn next.

QUESTIONS FOR REFLECTION AND DISCUSSION

1. Is *symbol* a positive or negative word for you?
2. How have you explained the death of Jesus?
3. Why is it important to recognize the crucifixions of our age? Where do you see crucifixion today?
4. What does the image of a "suffering God" do for you and your daily walk with God? Does God's suffering "weaken" God for you or make God more meaningful?
5. Can there be love without suffering?

9
DO YOU
NEED
A NEW
BEGINNING?

When the sabbath was over, Mary Magdalene, and Mary the mother of James, and Salome bought spices, so that they might go and anoint him. And very early on the first day of the week, when the sun had risen, they went to the tomb. They had been saying to one another, "Who will roll away the stone for us from the entrance to the tomb?" When they looked up, they saw that the stone, which was very large, had already been rolled back. As they entered the tomb, they saw a young man, dressed in a white robe, sitting on the right side; and they were alarmed. But he said to them, "Do not be alarmed; you are looking for Jesus of Nazareth, who was crucified. He has been raised; he is not here. Look, there is the place they laid him. But go, tell his disciples and Peter that he is going ahead of you to Galilee; there you will see him, just as he told you." So they went out and fled from the tomb, for terror and amazement had seized them; and they said nothing to anyone, for they were afraid.

Mark 16:1–8

I recently saw a news report about an Army veteran named John Crabtree who had been receiving benefits from the government. Evidently he had been wounded in Vietnam and was now on permanent disability. One day, out of the blue, he received an official notification from the government of his *own* death. Needless to say, this was quite a shock!

Mr. Crabtree wrote the government a letter stating that he was indeed very much alive and would like to continue receiving his benefits. The letter did no good. He then tried calling the government. (Have you ever tried to call the government? This requires the patience of Job and the persistence of Noah!) The phone calls didn't change the situation either. Finally, as a last resort, the veteran contacted a local television station, which ran a human-interest story about his situation.

During the interview the reporter asked him, "How do you feel about this whole ordeal?" The veteran chuckled and said, "Well, I feel a little frustrated by it. After all, *have you ever tried to prove that you're alive?*"

That's a pretty good question for all of us. Could you prove that you are alive? Really, genuinely, deep-down alive? When was the last time you had an alive moment? Not the last time you took a breath or had your heart beat inside your chest, but the last time you felt yourself alive to your living, alive to your loving, deeply present with the gift of life itself?

In the Bible there are two words for *time*. One is the Greek word *chronos*, which means linear or 1-2-3 kind of time. We all have to live on *chronos* time. Be at work by 8:00 in the morning. Pick the kids up at the day care center by 6:00 in the evening. Don't forget church every Sunday morning at 11:00! That's *chronos* time. *Chronos* time moves us along in the everyday world of responsibilities.

But there's another kind of time. It's described by the word *kairos*. *Kairos* means depth time, meaningful time, time that goes deeply into who we are in our most mysterious soulfulness. *Kairos* is time beyond linear *chronos* time. It's a moment when time stands still, and we come face to face with wisdom or meaning or love. Sometimes this is called sacred time.

When my wife and I first started dating, we would stay out late, sometimes into the middle of the night. We would go for long walks on her mom and dad's farm or around the neighborhood of our college. Sometimes it would be freezing cold outside.

It didn't matter. Sometimes it would be drizzling rain. Who cared? Darkness didn't matter either. And time didn't matter because we were not on *chronos* time, but *kairos* time. We were having this sacred experience of being in love, discovering our destinies in each other's eyes, discovering our own inner soulfulness. It was one of the most alive moments in my entire life!

The resurrection of Jesus is about such moments of depth and meaning. The resurrection is the quintessential *kairos* moment.

I might as well start from the beginning and say what the resurrection of Jesus is *not* about. *The resurrection is not a proof of the divinity of Jesus or the validity of the Christian faith.* I know some have tried to prove that the resurrection literally, actually, historically happened, but the truth is, proving the resurrection really happened is a modern concern and was never much of a biblical matter. The Gospel writers never report how the resurrection occurred or what happened during the resurrection. They simply announce the good news that the story of God's love has not ended with the death of Jesus, but indeed Jesus continues to live through his followers. It's certainly fine to ask the question, "What literally happened to his body in the dawn hours of that first Easter morning?" But there is no conclusive answer in the Bible to that question.

I cannot help but be interested in the new information coming forth in science that, in my mind, makes such an occurrence more credible and intelligible than ever before. Was the resurrection a quantum change in reality? It is hard to say for sure. Yet, the fact remains that no one really knows what actually happened to Jesus' body at that first Easter. Besides, even if you prove that Jesus literally was raised from the dead, out of a tomb, his lifeless body animated again, the question still remains: "What transformation does that make inside *your* soul?"

Additionally, *the resurrection is not about life after death.* Now that may seem strange to you if you have gone to Sunday school class most of your life and were taught that since Jesus died and went to heaven, we too can go to heaven after we die. That idea of life after death usually gets translated, "If we will be nice and good people, then we will be able to go to heaven (or at least escape hell) after we pass from this world to the next." Surprisingly, life after death receives very little attention in the Bible. Old Testament scriptures barely mention it, and New Testament scriptures only allude to it, assuming that there is life after death, but rarely explaining it or defending it or using it as motivation to live the Christian life. Personally, I do believe that conscious existence continues after death, but I also recognize that is not the central meaning of the resurrection story.

The *kairos* nature of resurrection means that it is about eternity, but not eternity in the linear sense of that word. Eternity is now! In the present moment. In an experience of meaning. In a moment of grace. In a moment of depth. Eternity just is! This is why you don't have to wait until you die to be with God. *Heaven*—a word typically used to describe what it's like to be with God after death—doesn't start the day you stop breathing; it begins the day you start living! It is the *eternal now*. And that too is what resurrection is about. It is about being alive, awake, conscious, aware, fully human, and walking a destiny that God has for you. Eternity is living each day in God's *kairos* moment. I know this might sound a little peculiar, but I think it is central to the truth of the Christian faith—The resurrection is more about *you* than it is about *Jesus*!

The telling of the first Easter story is dramatic and illustrates exactly what I'm talking about.

By the time the first Easter morning rolled around the disciples were devastated. They had become followers of Jesus. They believed in him. Loved him. Trusted him. What they believed is hard to tell. It seems likely that they believed he would start an earthly political-religious movement that finally would defeat the Romans and deliver the nation of Israel to power. They found the teachings of Jesus compelling. Moreover, they found him compelling. Jesus must have had some touch, some energy, some presence that dramatically engaged his followers. He had the gift of empowering people and bringing them to wholeness. The disciples had seen Jesus heal others, but they knew that Jesus had healed them too. He had accepted them. He had connected them to God.

In the last week of Jesus' life, however, everything started to go wrong. Jesus went to Jerusalem. What was supposed to have been a celebration of the high Jewish holiday of Passover became a tragedy for Jesus and his followers. Events blurred. Jesus was betrayed by Judas. Sold out for thirty pieces of silver. There was the Last Supper. The praying in the garden. Jesus wanted the disciples to pray too, but they were too sleepy. Tears were shed. His bogus arrest. It appears the Roman authorities saw Jesus as a political threat and wanted to get rid of him before this Jesus movement got out of hand. The hideous mocking. The fake trial. The carrying of his cross. And, in the end, the murderous death of a good man upon a cross.

Some of the disciples stayed around with each other. Some fled. All were crushed with disappointment. On the day that Jesus was crucified something else died. What died were the disciples' hopes and dreams. Many believed that this time, this one named Jesus of Nazareth was God's anointed to lead Israel through the wilderness of Roman persecution and bring Israel to the promised land of national power. Yet, with each pounding nail that went into Jesus' hands and with each gasping breath that he took, something in them died.

I want to tell you about Barbara. I met Barbara at a retreat I led a few years ago. The retreat was held in April when the Kentucky dogwoods were coming into their brilliance and the daffodils were popping open with yellow splendor. Spring is a time for new beginnings. When I met Barbara the last thing she was feeling was spring. Her husband had left her a few months earlier. More than twenty-five years of marriage were gone. Children. The home. The building of a life together. It was over. She had been holding out some hope that her husband would come back and they could work things out, but she knew it was unlikely. She couldn't understand. "What's wrong with me? I'll do whatever it takes. What does he want from me? I knew we had problems, but I didn't think they were that serious. What about our vows? What about for better or worse?" These were her questions. What I remember about Barbara is that she cried off and on the entire weekend. She had virtually no self-esteem.

We all have endings. Some of them are big and life-altering like Barbara's. A husband leaves. A wife dies. A child commits suicide. A career closes prematurely. Some of them are daily and ordinary, but they are endings nevertheless. We move from one city to another, leaving behind good friends. A child goes away to college, and we feel a little empty inside. A daughter marries, and there is a feeling that something is ending. Endings happen—sometimes in extraordinary ways, sometimes in quiet daily ways. But make no mistake, they do happen.

Those early disciples were enduring the biggest ending of their lives. Jesus was now dead. And no words could quite capture the despair they felt.

It was this gnawing feeling of endings that woke Mary Magdalene, Mary the mother of James, and Salome early on Sunday and drove them through the dark streets of Jerusalem. They were going to the tomb of Jesus. Because of Sabbath laws Jesus had been buried hurriedly, and they wanted to prepare his body properly for his final resting. They carried spices and ointments and oils. As painful as it might be, they were prepared to have someone roll away the stone to the cave where he had been buried and then take his body and anoint it with the proper burial lotions. (Notice, the ones who went to the tomb were women. None of the men are around. I wish some of the churches that relegate women to a second-class status would hear the resurrection story again. Some of the most prominent early disciples were women, a sure indication that women should have a significant role in the life of the church today.)

As they come closer to the tomb they see the large stone already has been moved. Their first thought was probably: "Vandalism! They've already killed him, did they have to disgrace his dead body?" But they go closer. Closer. Closer they move toward the tomb in the morning light now breaking over the hills of Jerusalem. They peek inside the cave and see a figure—a man? an angel? It's hard to be sure. This person announces, "He has been raised!"

This is no ending at all! It felt like an ending, to be sure, but God's not finished writing this story. Jesus lives! His life is not a bloom falling off the tree; the bud is just beginning to open. It's not explained why or how it all happened; it's just announced. And those women who went to the tomb so slowly and solemnly in the dark silence of the early morning are now running back to tell the other disciples. Mark's ending is fantastic. He writes, "So they went out and fled from the tomb, for terror and amazement had seized them; and they said nothing to anyone, for they were afraid."

The resurrection story of Mark offers a variety of insights. I think it's significant that this presence of life was terrifying and amazing to these disciples. This kind of terror is not a bad experience. There is a kind of terror before that which is beautiful—an utter amazement. When's the last time, for example, you felt any wonder? When's the last time you stood in awe before life? Have you ever had a moment when you were so alive or felt yourself to be so loved that you were afraid? The resurrection is *kairos* time; it is the eternity that is now. In the movie *Grand Canyon* the final scene has the characters standing in awe of the majesty of the Grand Canyon, but what they see is more than the physical landscape, they are witnessing some experience of rebirth inside themselves.

There is resurrection all around us. Every day there is resurrection. Daily there are moments when life breaks through. Maybe we can't explain it or predict it or schedule it, but if we have eyes to see and hearts to feel, it is there. Awe. Wonder. Joy. It's in the eyes of someone you love. It's in the human stories of love triumphing over hate. It's in the presence of God enduring with us when we go through some of our little moments of dying.

What's amazing about Barbara is that one year later I led a retreat for this same group, and she was a participant again. This time she was different. She did have spring in her life. Her eyes sparkled. For the first time I saw she had a beautiful smile. It was as if she were a different person. One year before she was consumed with endings; now she was alive with beginnings. The year had not been easy for her, but the year had brought resurrection.

I asked her during the weekend, "What's changed between this year and last year?" She said: "Last year was the most difficult year of my life. I finally decided that I couldn't live like that anymore. I started praying again, trusting God again. It wasn't easy at first, but I did. And it's made all the difference in the world."

The resurrection in Barbara's life was not instantaneous, but it was real. There were dark nights before she discovered any morning light. But she found it. An ending became a beginning. In the midst of her story and our stories and the stories of the early disciples, there was and is fear and amazement, terror and wonder. New life does that to people.

James Agee wrote a beautiful novel several years ago titled *A Death in the Family*. The story is told from the delicate perspective of a little boy whose father was killed in an automobile accident. Agee tells about the bewilderment of that boy and his struggle to understand this awful ending. There is much tone and texture to the story. The smell of funeral flowers and the solemn calling of friends, all in the home of the boy, a Southern tradition before there were professional funeral homes. The story ends with the boy's attending his father's funeral.

As the service comes to an end the boy witnesses a miracle. A beautiful butterfly slowly flies into the open grave and lights softly upon the casket. The wings beat once. Twice. There is a perfect harmony with the silence of the moment. And then, as gently as it entered the earthy grave, it flies off into the sky. What a beautiful symbol of new life. What was an ending became a beginning.

I recently read that in the Nazi concentration camps where children were kept before they were taken to the gas chamber, the walls hold the artistic scratchings and drawings of those children. The one motif that was found over and over was that of the butterfly. Isn't that remarkable? A symbol of resurrection in the midst of one of the world's worst crucifixions.

I once visited the gardens of New Harmony, Indiana, where Paul Tillich, without a doubt the greatest theologian of the twentieth century, is buried. In the Tillich Garden there is inscribed in stone one of his most moving sayings: "Any event which points you to the presence of God is a miracle."

That's exactly what the disciples experienced on that first Easter morning. On that morning they discovered that love endures beyond death, that the mystery of presence is more real than the reality of hatred. Yes, the crucifixion made a statement, but the resurrection makes an even louder one. The disciples felt and experienced beyond any doubt that Jesus was still living. How it happened is unimportant. What happened is neither here nor there. What mattered most is that the reality of what they discovered in the earthly life of Jesus now continues in the presence of the living Christ.

I thought of resurrection when I learned that one of my favorite musical groups, the Paul Winter Consort, did a musical recording while taking a float trip on the Colorado River, which flows through the Grand Canyon. Some of you, perhaps, have taken trips on that river, which meanders lazily through that magnificent landscape. Talk about inspiration: if you can't feel close to God at the Grand Canyon, I'm not sure you can feel close to God anywhere. A visual image I have is that of the members of that musical group playing their songs while floating on the river. As they make a sharp bend in the river the boat disappears from sight. But even though you cannot see them, you can still hear their music echoing in the canyon.

I think that's the feeling of what happened in the resurrection. Jesus started a kind of divine music. It was a music for all persons, especially for those who had been told their entire lives that they were not worthy to hear the music. It was a clear song of compassion. A movement of acceptance. A symphony of love. The music played until that dark day on Friday when Jesus was crucified. The music, for the friends and disciples of Jesus, died that day. For three days and nights the music looked like it indeed had died. It looked as if hate and murder and jealousy and suspicion and death were going to have the last word.

Then just at the moment when it seemed there was no more music, a singular note of a new beginning was heard on Sunday morning. Soon the note became a trumpet blast. Then a song. Then a chorus. "Christ the Lord is risen!" was the music that ignited the hearts of the early disciples. It set them dancing. It exploded with joy across the sky. Were they terrified? Surely they were. Reinventing your life and starting all over and being given a second chance are terrifying. But they were also joyful and exciting. Being alive can scare you to death. But better to be in awe and alive than among the living who are hollow and empty on the inside of their souls.

Mark tells the story of a new beginning, and that new beginning is present every day. If you read the resurrection story and think of it as something that happened a long time ago, then you've already missed it. Resurrection is now. It is the eternal now. The *kairos* moment of God's presence. It is the divine love that awaits all of us. Look around, and find its signs. The world is filled with new-life indicators. A butterfly in a novel. A woman who finds life after divorce. The joy of genuine community in a church. Resurrection fills the air, and God's music plays for each of us who has ever had this feeling of wanting to begin life all over again. Resurrection may come slowly, but it does come. With every sunset, with every sunrise, with every human touch, with every act of compassion, resurrection breaks open in our lives.

Last summer I attended the dedication of a Habitat for Humanity house built in Louisville, Kentucky, by volunteers from various churches. It was a warm August evening. The sun was setting over the Ohio River, and a group of us gathered on the front porch of this beautiful little house. My friends Rick and Susan Vance led our church to work on this project. A few words of dedication were offered, then a prayer. The young African-American woman and her two children who were ready to move into their new home were present. The woman was asked if she would like to say anything. She looked embarrassed, obviously unaccustomed to public speaking. The two kids were smiling and pulling on her cotton dress. She looked at the crowd for a moment. After a long silence, her eyes brimming with tears, she said, "I just want to thank all of you for giving me a *chance*."

Can you see? Can you feel? That moment was a resurrection moment. The presence of Jesus was there, as it is everywhere when there is hope brought to a neighborhood or a singular human heart where there once was hopelessness.

To know and feel God's love is resurrection. The touch of love always brings us to new life. I liked the episode on the television show *Northern Exposure* when the freewheeling Chris, who worked as the disc jockey at the local radio station, had something of a life crisis. Chris always had assumed he would die early like his father and grandfather. One day his fear caused him just to walk out of the radio station and run away on his motorcycle. Maurice, who owned the radio station, was furious at Chris's immaturity and immediately fired him. In the midst of this crisis, however, Chris learned that he was not going to die young. Indeed, he was the picture of health, and if he would just take care of himself, he could live to be an old man. Chris eventually made his way back to his old job at the radio station, and Maurice rehired him. On his first day back on the air, Chris said, "Thanks to Maurice Minniefield for giving me a second, second chance."

That's not a bad description of God. When we feel we have reached a dead end or, as is the case with many of us, when we have created dead ends for ourselves, God gives us a "second, second chance." The writer Frederick Buechner was asked, "Have you been born again?" His answer touched upon the miracle of the resurrection when he replied, "I have been born again and again and again!" That's what the God of new beginnings does!

Notice how Mark ends his story of the resurrection. In fact, he ends the story with no ending at all. The women go back to the other disciples, terrified and afraid, and that's the ending of the story. No tidy "they lived happily ever after." No quick and contrived conclusion. This was Mark's literary way of leaving the story wide open.

What's the conclusion of the resurrection? Who knows? The conclusion and influence of the resurrection depend upon you and me. They depend upon what kind of new life energy flows through us. Is the resurrection true? Mark would say that we have to look inside the lives of the disciples, inside our own lives. If we can see love and compassion and the energy of life, then the resurrection is indeed true.

Through interactive video today you can see a movie, then through a computer select which ending you want to see. Strange? To be sure, but that kind of technology is here. We've all probably watched a movie and walked away thinking, "I can't believe it ended that way! I wanted this or that to happen." In some ways that's what Mark is dong with his ending/no-ending. You get to finish the story. You get to complete the novel. The movie ends by what people see in your life.

What does it mean to be a resurrection person? Even though it is completely inadequate, I would suggest the following practical essentials for the resurrection of Christ to be real in you:

1. Resurrection people live with hope and bring hope to others. Betty Ford, wife of former President Gerald Ford, had to check into a hospital for alcohol abuse. Her problems became well publicized, even to the extent of a treatment hospital being named in her honor. During her recovery she held on tight to one thought, "God, help me to remember that there's nothing you and I can't handle together." That's living with hope. Through her discovery of hope, she has courageously brought hope to others.

2. Resurrection people affirm and accept the lives of others. It's so easy to approach people with judgment or, worse, animosity. Jesus was about giving people who had no chance a chance. To keep the spirit of Jesus alive means we approach people with the gifts of tolerance, acceptance, and understanding. That doesn't mean we endorse everything they do or like everything about them. Affirming others means that we see their value in the world and that we seek to treat them as human beings should be treated.

3. Resurrection people are inviting people. One way Christians reach out to people who are not connected with the faith is by inviting them to their church. I teach a newcomers class at my church. When I go around and ask the class members, "How did you get started worshiping here?"—the answer is almost always, "Someone here invited me." I'll never forget John who joined our church a few years ago. I asked him why he had never joined a church until now. The obviousness of his answer startled me: "Because no one ever asked me to." If you want to lead people to Christ, the best way is not to beat people over the head with your religion. Instead, simply invite them to church. The Spirit will do the work from there.

4. Resurrection people are in touch with the mystery of presence. Is this elusive feeling of presence that resurrection people finally touch and are touched by Mystery? Mystery is feeling the presence of God as it expresses itself in daily life. I recall moments in life of feeling this mysterious presence. Sometimes it is a moment of nature. At other times it is in the poetry of relationships. Living the resurrection means feeling the mystery of God in all places.

5. Resurrection people bring new beginnings to others. It's one thing to feel God's giving us a new beginning; it's another to make your mission in life to help others find one too. Think of the number of people you meet each day. The waitress at the local restaurant. The man working at the toll booth each morning. The crossing guard near the school. The teller at your bank. Every single day we meet people, and each of those encounters is an opportunity to pass on a new beginning. It might be a kind word. It might be an affirming note of gratitude regarding their job performance. It might be just a smile. Even more pointedly, when you forgive someone or let go of a grudge or release an old ax you've been grinding for years, you give someone else a new beginning.

Think about it one more time. *If you had to prove to someone you were alive, how would you do it?*

"He is risen" were the words that echoed forth from that first Easter experience, and those words still come alive. They come alive again and again when the resurrection happens inside us, when we let God give us the new beginning we need, and when we pass on that new beginning to others. To begin again is the mark of resurrection people and the beginning of the spiritual adventure God calls us to live.

QUESTIONS FOR REFLECTION AND DISCUSSION

1. Name one of the most alive moments in your existence. What do alive moments of different people have in common?
2. There is a difference between *chronos* and *kairos*. How would you describe *kairos* moments, and what can you do to have more *kairos* time in your life?
3. If you had to tell a story about a resurrection that you have seen in your life or in the life of another, what would that story be? It's easy to find crucifixion in the world, but sometimes harder to name resurrection. Where do you see God at work bringing new life?
4. Have you ever had a life ending that became a significant beginning?
5. Mark ends his story with an ending that is not an ending. How is God right now trying to write the story of resurrection in your life?

IV

SPIRIT

10
HAVE YOU
FOUND
THE CREATIVE
FIRE?

In the beginning when God created the heavens and the earth, the earth was a formless void and darkness covered the face of the deep, while a wind from God swept over the face of the waters. Then God said, "Let there be light"; and there was light. And God saw that the light was good; and God separated the light from the darkness. God called the light Day, and the darkness he called Night. And there was evening and there was morning, the first day.

Genesis 1:1–5

The creation story from the book of Genesis invites imagination. It's too bad the word *imagination* has come to mean "make-believe" or "fabrication." The truth is, imagination is deeply related to the experience of faith. To imagine—or to create images of spiritual realities—requires a great deal of trust, and trust is faith. At the same time, images have the power to become sacraments, imparting to our lives grace and hope.

When I imagine this reading from Genesis, I think of the deep darkness of space. What do the words cause you to imagine? Read them again and again and let the gift of your imagination work. I imagine a night sky so deep and dark that it looks and feels endless. If you've ever been to Mammoth Cave in Kentucky, you probably remember that at a certain point on the tour, the lights are turned out and you just stand in the darkest of dark space.

I imagine the beginning as darkness. And then, if you somehow penetrate the darkness with your sight, you would begin to see a glob of floating dirt and water hanging out in space. Mud. Chaotic, formless, floating mud. At some places on this floating chaos there is more water than mud, at other places more mud than water. This is a floating flood. Everything running in all directions. Wild and free and full of potential. Some scientists have called it the cosmic soup.

Isn't it interesting that in the Bible's creation story there is the presence of matter? *Something* is there. The idea that God created something out of nothing is not really a concept associated with this creation story. God creates out of something. And that something begins to change and transform and, yes, evolve.

It's unfortunate that the word *evolve* has become so negative with some Christians. I can appreciate the fact that Christians try to defend the validity and truth of the Bible. I want to do the same myself. The conflict of "evolutionism" versus "creationism" was set up years ago and, in the minds of many, continues to be an unresolvable contradiction.

From my perspective, this is a false and completely unnecessary conflict. The creation story of the Bible was never meant to be a scientific account of how the world started. This is not a journalistic account of what really happened! The very idea of science was not present when Genesis was written. Was the world actually created in six twenty-four-hour days? Did God literally sit down and rest on the seventh day? Is Genesis meant to give a total explanation of how the earth got going? Someone once came to me all disturbed and asked, "What about the dinosaurs?"

The irrefutable facts—not theories, but facts—uphold the idea that the world has and continues to evolve. To evolve simply means to change, and change is exactly what the story of creation is about. Sometimes the changes are dramatic; usually they are minute and beyond the naked eye. But the world is constantly changing, and change is the work of the Holy Spirit in the world. The discoveries of science do nothing but support the "evolutionary-creationary-changing" nature of the universe. Regardless of the theory of how the world came into being, the presence of God was and is part of the creative changing of the cosmos.

The theological insight in this biblical story is that God is the energy, the presence, the fire that turns the wheels of this changing, transforming, ever-becoming universe. While this chaotic mud ball is floating out in the darkness of space, there is another presence, a presence called Spirit or wind. In Hebrew the word is *ruach*, which literally means breath. It is a wonderful image of God's breath moving across the dark waters of chaos. The Spirit of God was moving and hovering and searching and stirring over the waters of chaos, and through this Spirit or divine energy the world began to change and be created.

In light of this story of God's creative Spirit, the question before each Christian is: *What is the work of the Holy Spirit in our lives?*

I think at the heart of the Spirit's work in our daily living is the experience of creativity. Sometimes this idea of Spirit is peculiar to us as Christians. When we think of Spirit, we may imagine a wild Pentecostal meeting with people fainting, speaking in tongues, and shouting out praises to God. That is one way to think of Spirit, but it seems to me that there are other ways of understanding the work and presence of the Spirit in a Christian's life.

Simply stated, the Holy Spirit is the presence of divine creative energy in the life of a Christian. The Spirit is that inner presence within us that assures us we are not alone. The Spirit is a strength beyond our own strength. The Spirit is sometimes a spiritual feeling—a feeling of being close to God or maybe an experience of life flow, one of those moments when life is full and strong and beautiful. The Spirit is mysterious, but that does not mean it is nonsense. The Spirit is elusive, but that does not mean it cannot be understood. It is not the case that some Christians have the Spirit and some do not. The Spirit is not a reward reserved for spiritual superstars and withheld from "regular" Christians. The Spirit is a gift to everyone who confesses faith in Jesus Christ.

What might it look like if we experience the creativity of the Holy Spirit in our everyday lives? Creativity is that wonderful feeling of looking at life in a new way, expressing some vision of our lives, approaching a situation in a different and novel way. The presence of the Holy Spirit throughout the creation of the world called forth newness! The Bible's emphasis on newness is well known. Christians are born anew. Christians are called to be God's new creation. The final vision for the universe is a new heaven and new earth. Newness and creativity are part of the wonderful work of the Spirit.

Are you a creative person? If you're like most people the answer is a quick, "Oh no, I'm not creative. Why, I don't paint or sing or play any kind of musical instrument. I could never do that!"

And with words like that we tend to diminish our creativity. Unfortunately, most of us associate creativity with artistry. It is true that not everyone can be a professional artist. There is, after all, only one Mozart or Beethoven. Only one Picasso or Renoir. Artists who express their creativity and receive professional recognition for their created works are few and far between. But creativity is much larger than professional artistry. Everyone can be creative, and the experience of creativity is an experience of the Spirit.

I was teaching a class of young adults not long ago, and I started our session with this very question, "Are you a creative person?" There were thirty people in the group. Yet only one person raised her hand in response to possessing creativity. Obviously, everyone in the group had imagined creativity only in terms of being artistic. And by the way, the one who raised her hand was a professional portrait artist.

I then asked them, "What are ways we can express our creativity in daily life?" Slowly the answers began to flow.

"Helping solve a problem at work," one nurse said.

"Listening to someone in a special way," another person suggested.

"Taking care of my two toddlers all day," one mother said to the cheers of all the other parents in the room.

The suggestions went on. "Listening to music." "Playing music." "Gardening." "Preparing a nice dinner." "Decorating the house." "Going out to eat." "Shopping, finding that right gift for that special person." "Playing golf." (That one was mine!) "Finding ways of making relationships better." "Working effectively with difficult people." (I think that one was my wife's!) "Writing poetry." "Painting." "Landscaping." "Singing in the choir." "Doing a good job teaching." "Helping patients." "Putting together project plans." By the end of our hour together we must have brainstormed fifty ways of being creative. It was a great moment of creativity just talking about creativity.

Creativity is the work of the Holy Spirit. To be open to creative energy is to be open to the Spirit.

Now, I'm aware that you might be thinking: "Well, that doesn't seem very religious. I thought the Spirit would be, well, more *spiritual.*"

I can understand that response. For many of us religion has come to be associated with doing explicitly religious or church things. At the same time, I would encourage you to begin thinking that maybe faith is about doing ordinary things in such a way that even the ordinary becomes extraordinary—extraordinarily religious and spiritual. The simple baking of a loaf of bread with its wonderful aroma and crusty skin and delicious taste can be an experience of creativity. When an ordinary task is done with a degree of mindfulness and love, that can become a spiritual moment. The psalmist declared long ago, "The earth is the Lord's and the fullness thereof." That was a way of saying that everything in the world is infused with the presence of God and what's needed is the creative heart to hear it, taste it, touch it, feel it, and see it. The poet Gerard Manley Hopkins stated it best when he wrote, "The world is charged with the grandeur of God." This is what Walt Whitman meant when he declared that he would "sing the body electric." Everything is alive and charged with the presence of God!

In a recent presentation on PBS there was a discussion of creativity. In that program the participants offered some excellent ways to enhance creativity and thus create more experience of the Spirit.

The first suggestion was to *dare to be naive.* On the one hand, naïveté can be dangerous. People who are naive get into trouble, are taken advantage of, and find themselves in situations in which they never should have been. On the other hand, naïveté means looking at the world with fresh eyes. Maybe you've driven down a road a thousand times, but the naive eye seeks to see the trees along the road in a new way. Really see the trees! Maybe even pull the car over, stand beside the tree, and reach out and touch the bark of the tree. That's daring to be naive.

Pablo Picasso once said, "I spent the first half of my life trying to become an adult, the second half trying to become a child." Naïveté is not stupidity. Nor is it make-believe. It is, however, the exercise of faith and imagination to see life differently or perhaps to see the life that you've been missing all along. I think this element of naïveté may be exactly what Jesus was getting at when he said, "You must become like a little child." He wasn't endorsing immaturity. There's too much of that in the world as it is! He was daring people to find the childlike eye in order to see God more clearly. Sadly, for many of us, growing up has come to mean losing our capacity to see and feel. I think it's fascinating that scientists are now saying that every person has an IQ and an EQ. Our EQ is our emotional capacity to feel, imagine, and be alive.

In our professions we especially need to rediscover naivete. We become so familiar with our law practice or our teaching methods or our way of delivering sermons that we become stagnant, boring, stale. It is startling to learn the number of people who are unhappy with their work. We feel stuck. We feel bored. We daydream of escaping to something more exciting and fulfilling. In our work we especially need freshness. We need perspective. Many times what we need is not a new job, but new eyes for the old job. And the way to discover that is to take on the childlike eye and begin living with the naïveté to see things anew. I think one of the most profoundly spiritual experiences we could ever have is finding new creativity and spirit in our daily work.

Another suggestion for creativity is *to be playful and delightful.* How many of our marriages have become heavy industry? How many of us think of work only as hard, laboring drudgery? At one time the concept of home meant a place of rest, renewal, and refreshment. Today, many of our homes have become just as demanding and organized as the office. I notice that even those lucky folks who go on vacations often come back exhausted and drained, not the least bit refreshed, and then start back at their work without any creativity or energy.

When I read the creation story of the Bible, I see playfulness. Take a look at this big, beautiful, humorous world God created. Have you ever taken a good look at an anteater? Or a hippopotamus? Or a giraffe? Somebody had a pretty good sense of humor just to be playful enough to bring it all together. The story of creation is really a song, a poem that, in and of itself, reflects the playful, delightful nature of God. I like to think of God singing the world into existence and then giving man and woman the ultimate playground—the lush, green, fruitful garden named *Eden*, a word that means pleasure. At the heart of God and at the heart of this complex universe is joy, and, when we open ourselves to that deep-down joy, we find pure delight.

I would urge anyone who wants to get closer to God to find ways of incorporating into his or her life moments of playfulness and delight. That's not to say that we should make recreation a little god as many seem to do in our culture. Our culture has become entertainment driven and recreationally saturated. I mourn the loss of genuine play and authentic sport to a culture that has made play big business, athletics entertainment, and vacation serious adventure. Genuine human play should never be confused with the entertainment craze that bounces all around us. To experience play is to be open to the energy of the Spirit. Ask yourself: *"When was the last time I played? When was the last time I felt playful with another human being? When was the last time I just let go and started to sing or dance or laugh?"* To play is to love God again!

Another element of creativity is *risk*. Every time a potter begins to feel the clay in her hands and spin her well-worn potter's wheel there is risk. Cutting flowers and arranging them in a vase is risk. Painting a picture, playing an instrument, writing a poem, offering a new direction for the company in a wood-paneled boardroom is risky business. Yet creativity demands risk. I'm sure that I have wadded up and thrown away literally thousands of pieces of paper as I have written sermons and articles and poems over the years. But finally to send something to a publisher and let someone else read it is very risky!

The risk is that you might absolutely flop in your creative attempt. I recently read that after Abraham Lincoln gave the Gettysburg Address he sat down and whispered to a friend that he thought it was the worst speech he had ever given. Sometimes creative attempts feel like failures. Often I have gone home after preaching a sermon wanting to hide my head in the sand like an ostrich because I felt my attempt at creativity was a flop. The actor Tom Hanks told Larry King recently that he has learned more from his movie flops than his movie successes. The risk of failure is real, but there is no creativity without failure.

Part of our feeling of failure comes from an inner voice, an inner critic that crouches down in our soul and is always ready to pounce upon us and say:

"Oh, you're not very talented."

"Why are you trying to sing in the choir? Everyone else is probably better."

"Don't even waste your time trying to fix a nice meal. You can't cook."

"Look at that painting. The colors are all wrong."

Have you ever heard the voice of that harsh critic? The inner critic can be hateful, mean, degrading to your soul, and demonic. Some of us had a mother or father who was a harsh critic, and that voice still echoes inside us. It is the voice that in one way or another communicates to us that we are *not enough*.

One day while I was hiking in the Ventana wilderness in California, I found a little waterfall that emptied into the Pacific. I was struck by the vastness of the ocean and the smallness of this little stream. It inspired this poem, which I entitled "Enough Is Enough," and for me it is about the process of creativity:

> *This stream*
> *Emptying*
> *Into the Pacific*
> *Does not weep*
> *That it is not*
> *Enough.*

It should be said that some critical voice is necessary for our lives. Criticism and honest self-observation can help us become more effective with our creativity. If I try to paint and the colors or technique don't really come off very well, my inner critic can say something like, "I don't think this really works. No big deal. We'll just do it better next time." The parents we had usually set the stage for much of our creativity as adults. If you had a mother or father who was supportive and affirming to you as a child, then you probably can be self-critical in a positive way. All people need an encouraging person in their lives, especially children. Yet, no doubt all of us, at one time or another, have sat and wept at our not being enough.

The other piece of the failure picture is that often someone is around us who is ready to criticize and make us feel like failures in our creative attempts. Managers are especially prone to do this. It is too easy to squelch the creative attempts of those who work under us. Frequently a spouse will do this. I know a woman who wanted to learn to play tennis. However, her husband did nothing but make fun of her and offer snide remarks about the prospect of her taking up this sport. She came home after her first lesson, and he said, "Well, are you ready for Wimbledon? Did you fall in love with the tennis pro? How many times did you trip on the court today?" Do you see what he was doing? He was trying to murder her creativity. I encouraged her to stay with her creativity because I knew for her it was a spiritual attempt to reach God and a deeper authenticity in her living.

I think we can risk failure when we understand that the Spirit is worth it. Faith is the courage, the daring, the nerve to reach beyond where we are and become what God is calling us to be. Easy? Not usually. Scary? Sometimes. Worth it? Always!

Martin Luther, the great Reformation theologian, would say it like this, "Sin boldly!" By that expression Luther was not encouraging sin. Instead, he believed so much in God's grace to forgive us when we might make a mistake that he encouraged Christians to live fully and confidently and, yes, risk failure, all the time knowing that God will never fail to pick us up. I love the expression of Alfred North Whitehead who said, "It is the business of the universe to be dangerous!" There is no creativity without risk.

Another part of creativity is the idea of *opening the door to flow*. If you have never experienced flow, then this may seem like a strange concept. However, if you have had a moment when you felt as if you were at one with God or at one with the universe, or have had a moment when you felt totally at peace, at home, connected to the deepest place inside your soul, then you know something about flow. Flow is related to what Abraham Maslow called "peak experience." A peak experience is one of extreme aliveness, extreme gratefulness—an experience when you feel yourself crying out: "Yes! Yes, this is who I really am. This is why I am on this earth. This is what life is all about!"

Part of what happens in flow experiences is that we feel ourselves creatively energized. I have, for example, played rounds of golf when I found myself playing poorly. My mind was somewhere else. By the time I reached the thirteenth hole I was wishing I was anywhere except on a golf course. On the other hand, I have had rounds of golf—not a lot of them, mind you, but a few of them—when I felt the beauty and mystery of golf play right through my body. My swing was in a groove. I was making good decisions about shots. I was hitting my putts, and the hole looked as big as a bushel basket. It was a round of golf characterized by intense vividness and aliveness. It was flow.

Most artists will tell you that any artistic expression is hard work. They might make it look easy, but it is hard work. Yet, artists also will tell you that there are peak moments when they stop consciously moving the brush and the brush moves them or the words just flow or the project comes together with crystal clarity or energy comes through so magnificently that they wonder where the words came from. I have a friend who is president of his own company and becomes extremely energized when meetings go well, especially those meetings that go better than he ever imagined. The personalities, the ideas, the possibilities all flow and blend together. He loves those flow moments. Being open to the flow of creativity is being open to the flow of the Spirit.

When I was in high school, I had the privileged nightmare of playing basketball against Larry Bird. He was a year ahead of me in school and was one of the best high school basketball players ever to come out of southern Indiana. I remember guarding him and having that helpless feeling that there was nothing I could do to stop him from scoring. I think he scored more than fifty points against us that night. (By the way, my coach congratulated me for a good defensive effort!) I watched Larry Bird have an incredible flow night. He later would go on and have more flow nights against Magic Johnson and Michael Jordan, leading the Boston Celtics to many wins. But he was at his best when the game of basketball was mystically playing him and not his playing basketball.

Be open to flow. Be open to the flow of your creative experiences. You may not have flow every day, but when it happens, it is a God-moment and should be enjoyed and relished. There is flow at the ocean, in the mountains, at the desert. Flow also can be discovered in the office or at church or in your home. The key to flow is oneness.

If openness is important to the Spirit's flow, then the final element of creativity I would offer to you is *the practice of letting go*. A middle-aged man, John, came into my office a few weeks ago. I had seen him at church some, but he came in this day to tell me his story. He'd been involved in a life-and-death struggle with alcohol. Not easy. He'd been attending Alcoholics Anonymous regularly. Again, not easy—especially attending your first AA meeting. Some of the people I admire most in this world are recovering alcoholics. I admire their strength and courage, their relentless desire to rediscover their lives and find well-being again. I also admire their unashamed confession that they need to rely on a "Higher Power." This attitude of letting go and relying on God is at the heart of faith.

John said to me: "It's at once liberating and scary to give up running my life. I now try to stay focused on every day, and that's all I can do."

All I could do was affirm the deep insight he was trying to incorporate. It does take faith to let go of trying to do everything in our lives, to let go of much of the perfection that drives so many of us. But in letting go we open ourselves to the flow of God's Spirit.

In terms of creativity, many of us try to steer our way through life by doing what we've always done, what has come naturally, or what comes to us by virtue of habit. But part of creativity means we trust that what needs to flow will flow. Letting go, for example, of the need to turn out a perfect painting, and just painting for the sheer joy of it. Letting go of the need to sing so that someone else approves of our singing, and just singing for the personal ecstasy it brings to our lives. Letting go of dressing to please our spouse, and buying the tie or the dress or the hat or the jacket that touches our soulful creativity, becomes a genuine act of faith. Letting go is not easy, but it is essential.

I see this with folks in the church who feel as if they know so little about the Bible or about theology that they stay away from opportunities that could indeed enhance their knowledge. I try to tell people that the first step to growing as a Christian is just not caring how much you're growing. Don't care! Let go of the feeling that you might be stupid. This kind of spiritual self-consciousness has to be let go, released, surrendered. It takes a lot of trust to live, but as the apostle Paul said again and again, "We walk by faith and not by sight."

I'm intrigued by this idea of becoming a novice. A few years ago my son and I wanted to learn to fly fish. I had a friend who was a pretty good fly fisherman, and so he started taking Matthew and me with him.

On our way to our first outing my son asked, "Dad, have you ever fly fished before?"

I said, "No. I used to fish as a kid, but I've never fly fished."

He thought for a minute and then said, "I like it that we are going to learn together. That kind of makes us equals."

What he saw was not the terror, but the delight of being a novice, a learner. Letting go of expertise and learning a new skill can be an experience of the Spirit. And that's important because it takes a great deal of faith to learn a new skill. When fly fishing, if you try to muscle the line and the little fly out into the water, it is nothing but disaster. All the muscle and effort will fail. What's needed is letting go and trusting. The flex of the rod will do the work. The weight of the line will carry the small fly several yards right to the spot where the fish are, or at least should be. Becoming a novice in any creative enterprise will teach you about faith and trust and the difficulty and delight of letting go.

It might be helpful to your Christian life to answer some creative call or creative endeavor that has been pressing itself upon you. Give it a try! Become a novice. Learn a new skill. Let go. Open up. To go through the experience of letting go is to walk into the room of the Spirit.

Creativity. It is the stuff of humanity. It is the work of the Holy Spirit. When a person tunes in to the experience of creativity, then the Spirit begins doing its brooding, hovering, wind-swept breathing over our lives. Just as in the beginning when oozing mud hung chaotically in space and God breathed upon it and the days started to unfold in cosmic beauty, so the Spirit wants to do that work again and again. Don't get caught up in the misconception that "spiritual" means always doing something "churchy." Church is important. But the essential work of the Spirit is to help us find voice for our most authentic selves, providing meaning for our most ordinary lives. You don't have to go to school to find creativity. You don't have to be formally educated to have creative energy. Instead, what's needed is openness, faith, courage, awareness, and a willingness to be led by the Spirit.

QUESTIONS FOR REFLECTION AND DISCUSSION

1. If you're in a group, go around the room and tell in the most imaginative way possible the story of the creation.
2. Is the use of "imagination" a part of your daily life? Why are we not more imaginative people? Write a list of imagination blockers in your life.
3. Can you recall a time in your life when you really felt creative? Do you ever feel that way now? What could you do to enhance your creativity?
4. We all have this inner, negative critic that wants to destroy our creativity. What does your inner critic say to you? How can you learn to tell your inner critic to "shut up"?
5. Have you ever had a moment when you had to "let go" and deeply trust God? When was it? What did it feel like?

11
ARE YOU
LIVING
WITH
HOPE?

For all who are led by the Spirit of God are children of God. For you did not receive a spirit of slavery to fall back into fear, but you have received a spirit of adoption. When we cry, "Abba! Father!" it is that very Spirit bearing witness with our spirit that we are children of God, and if children, then heirs, heirs of God and joint heirs with Christ—if, in fact, we suffer with him so that we may also be glorified with him.

I consider that the sufferings of this present time are not worth comparing with the glory about to be revealed to us. For the creation waits with eager longing for the revealing of the children of God; for the creation was subjected to futility, not of its own will but by the will of the one who subjected it, in hope that the creation itself will be set free from its bondage to decay and will obtain the freedom of the glory of the children of God. We know that the whole creation has been groaning in labor pains until now; and not only the creation, but we ourselves, who have the first fruits of the Spirit, groan inwardly while we wait for adoption, the redemption of our bodies. For in hope we were saved. Now hope that is seen is not hope. For who hopes for what is seen? But if we hope for what we do not see, we wait for it with patience.

*Likewise the Spirit helps us in our weakness; for we do not
know how to pray as we ought, but that very Spirit intercedes with sighs too deep for words. And God, who searches
the heart, knows what is the mind of the Spirit, because
the Spirit intercedes for the saints according to the will of
God.*

Romans 8:14–27

Part of what it means to experience the Spirit is to experience
hope. Hope is not just a nice, religious, church-type word. Instead, it is at the heart of what it means to live life fully and richly.
One of the best gifts of the church is that it calls people to live
hopefully, often contrary to the materialism and despair that per-
meate our culture.

When I look at young people today, it doesn't matter to me
whether they go to a prestigious school or what career they pursue
or how much money they finally will accumulate over a lifetime.
What matters is: Will they live life with hope? Will they discover
the deep-down feeling inside their soul that their life matters? Will
they have a eureka moment of discovery that they have something
to contribute to this world? These are the essential questions of
hope.

I was driving through a small Indiana town a few years ago,
and I saw an old game arcade that had been shut down. The glitzy
sign still hung above the door, holding forth the promise of fun
and entertainment. But the windows had been boarded up, and
cheap letters on the door spelled out the message: "OUT OF BUSI-
NESS." However, spray painted across that message and scrawled
across the boarded-up windows was some teenager's cry of hurt
and, who knows, maybe even a cry for help: "WE ARE BORED!!!"
Boredom. Meaninglessness. Emptiness. These are cries for hope.

Recently Harvard University was rocked to its core when
officials discovered two students had committed a double suicide
in their dormitory room. When I think of Harvard, I think of the
best and brightest young people in the world attending classes in
ivy-covered buildings. Young adults readying themselves to go out
into the world in order to accomplish much. But regardless of the

prestige of the place, unless there is hope—hope inside the human heart that assures people that they are not alone in this world and that their lives matter and that life is worth living—the best homes or schools or companies become only hollow shells or decorated prisons.

In this reflection text from the book of Romans, Paul is addressing the issue of hope. It's interesting how his thought develops. If you have never read the book of Romans, I would encourage you to do so. It gets a little dense at times, but don't let that intimidate you. Plow through it, and what you will find is complex and rich theological reasoning.

Paul begins the book by painting a picture of the human situation. You might title this portrait "All the Broken Pieces." As human beings we do have this sense that life is fragmented, that life isn't working quite right, that there is something missing. In Paul's language, "All have sinned and fall short of the glory of God" (Romans 3:23).

I would suggest that you not think of sin simply as doing wrong things. Surely that's part of it, but sin is much more. Sin is something of a state we are in. It is a state of being, a condition of life's breaking into pieces. We may not be doing something wrong per se, but we still have this awful, nagging feeling that something is wrong, very wrong, with our lives. We may try to keep that disturbing news to ourselves. We may become masterful at masking it or covering it up or decorating it so that others can't see into our private suffering. But in our most honest moments we know without any doubt that we are sinners in the sense of being unwhole, fragmented, split-off people. The poet Tomas Transtromer drove home the point in poignant fashion when he wrote: "I see you have a beautiful house. The ghetto must be in your heart." I would guess there is a ghetto inside every human heart.

I was talking with a family a few weeks ago. I could hear in their words and feelings something of this brokenness. This family had been the all-American family. The father had a good career. The mother is one of the brightest, wittiest, funniest people I have ever been around. Their daughters are all attractive, now married, living life on their own. One daughter, however, recently has gone through a living hell with a husband who is out of control. He had become a drug user. Financial mismanagement was also part of the picture. An awful custody battle for their one child was whirling around the entire family. This whole family, which for years had looked picture-perfect, was now unraveling.

The mother, who had been trying to help her daughter and grandchild, looked at me one day in the hallway at church and said, "This kind of thing doesn't happen to people like us. I mean, it's worse than a soap opera. I can't believe it's happening."

Her deep human cry, her utter feeling of dismay, is not just her cry. It is your cry and my cry and the cry of any person who has walked the earth. It's not a matter of committing sin, though I'm sure we all do our part in that category. It is that we are all participants in a world that is always falling apart. No wonder we always are in need of the new beginnings that the resurrection of Jesus offers.

Paul, in fact, writes in the book of Romans that "the whole creation has been groaning" (Romans 8:22). Maybe you have never felt this kind of painful groaning, but my guess is you have or at least someone you know has. Seeing pictures of a war-torn Bosnia is a kind of groaning, as are pictures of starving children in Somalia, overdeveloped lands along the coastal waters of this country, and wandering homeless people in New York City. The whole creation is groaning. That's what it means to be a sinner. Being a sinner does not mean you are a shameful, bad, awful person; it means you are part of a picture that is fundamentally in trouble and needs help.

Well, that's the bad news that Paul delivers in Romans. However, he doesn't leave us there. Aren't you glad? He moves into the area of faith and grace and the joy of the presence of God in a world breaking into pieces. This section of Romans might be labeled "God Picks Up the Pieces."

God's putting pieces together is really the meaning of salvation. Salvation is not so much envisioned by Paul as something we get at the end of life, like a reward for being good. Salvation has very little to do with our own goodness, and it certainly is not a reward we earn by racking up spiritual brownie points. Salvation is recognizing that God is a God of radical love—a deep-down-to-the-bone, never-leave-or-never-waver, stay-with-us-forever kind of love. That message of love was expressed in the person of Jesus Christ, in his life and death and resurrection, and continues to be expressed to the world through the ministry of the church.

Through Jesus Christ, people like you and me have a chance to see what God is really like—pure 100 percent love! To be saved, according to Paul, means we have discovered faith in Jesus Christ who is the supreme expression of God's love and God's acceptance of us. Even though we have sinned or, better said, even though we all are broken, God loves us. Even though the world is falling apart, God loves us. Even though we do things that are totally unacceptable, God accepts us. This is the gift and beauty of the Christian faith.

What Jesus did in his ministry was to tell stories that helped people both comprehend and experience God as a God of love. He told the story, for example, of a son who had drifted away from his family, but decided to come home. When the father saw the vagabond boy, he jumped out of his porch rocker like a sprinter blasting out of the blocks, ran down the dusty lane with breakneck speed, threw his arms around the lost son, kissed him with joy, and sprinkled his face with tears of happiness. And if that weren't enough, he threw the boy a big, boisterous bash! A party. How's that for a picture of what God is like? Being with God is like being at a party twenty-four hours a day, and you—not God, but *you*—are the guest of honor! That's remarkable love.

And Jesus told the story of a group of poor people who used to look at the castle of the king and wistfully dream of just getting a glimpse inside the palatial mansion or having the king say a personal "hello" as he passed along the street. On this special day, however, the king rejects all the rich and powerful people and invites all the poor and weak people to the wedding reception of his son, the prince. A wonderful wedding party ensues. Can you imagine it? Here these folks could think of the king only as a distant, unattainable, impersonal force, but now because of his remarkable generosity, they are brought into the palace of their dreams and are made to feel like royalty. That's remarkable acceptance.

There is suffering in the world to be sure. But the Christian faith is about seeing and experiencing God as one who loves and heals our broken lives. We do not suffer alone. God is the companion who through all our ups and downs endures with us. This is why the Christian message was called the *gospel*. The word *gospel* means *good news*! Maybe all the king's horses and all the king's men could not put Humpty-Dumpty back together again, but God can and does put people back together, does this every day because love is finally what makes us whole. Love is the strongest glue in the world.

The two words that Paul uses the most to help people understand the good news of God are *faith* and *grace*. Both are indispensable.

Faith is a powerful word, though it is one that often is misunderstood. For most of us, faith has come to mean "beliefs" or certain "ideas" that we have come to believe to be true. For example, someone might ask me, "Do you believe in the Trinity? Do you believe in the divinity of Jesus? Do you believe in heaven and hell?" When I'm asked those kinds of questions, I understand what the person is trying to do. I appreciate the kind of answer he or she is after. The person, typically, is asking me if I agree with a certain concept. More often than not, the person wants to know if I agree with her or him. However, this is not the only way to use "faith" or "belief."

When Paul uses the word *believe*, he means much more than simply agreeing with a concept. You might agree with a concept but never have your heart changed. This happens for people who have gone to church for years but have never found an experiential life change for themselves. Church is not about keeping certain beliefs going; church is about finding spiritual insight and renewal. For Paul, faith means putting confidence in something, trusting, depending, relying, placing some person or idea at the center of your life. Crossing the Golden Gate Bridge means having faith or confidence that the engineers and builders constructed a bridge that will do its job. Flying in a jet plane across the Atlantic Ocean demands a kind of faith in plane builders, maintenance crews, and pilots—faith that all of them will do the job to get you from one place to another. When children grow up and go away to college, you have to trust that they will make healthy decisions, that they will take care of themselves, that they will move in directions that will be for their best and most wholesome interest. You finally have to let go and put faith in them.

Faith in God means believing that God will love us without condition or hesitancy. It is finally that gift of love that saves and brings wholeness to our lives. This experience of God's unconditional love is sometimes referred to by Paul as a gift of grace.

Grace is not so much a doctrine or an idea that you *believe in* as it is a way of understanding and experiencing God. It is an orientation toward God. A relationship. Often I see people trying to approach their faith as a system of beliefs. They work very hard at getting all the beliefs in the right place, in the right order, every dimension of the Bible perfectly in relation to the others. Yet, this has never been the true heart of the Christian faith. Grace is a way of seeing all of life as a gift. It is an orientation toward God that is a relationship adventure.

If you've ever had someone in your life who believed in you, accepted you unconditionally as a person, and constantly gave your life meaning and affirmed your potential in this world, then you have experienced grace. Maybe it was a mother or father. Perhaps an aunt or grandmother or grandfather. A best friend. These are the people who have the power to witness to the giftedness of our own lives and the giftedness of the world itself. These are relationships of grace.

From the perspective of Paul, the gospel is about finding a relationship of grace with the God of the universe. Not God as a hard-hearted judge looking to catch us doing things that are wrong. Not God as a cosmic gambler, sometimes helping us, sometimes not. Not as a distant, punishing God who disdains our brokenness. Instead, God is offering authentic relationship to everyone, and it is always—not sometimes, but always—a relationship of grace. Yes, our suffering remains. That's where the Spirit comes in. But there's grace in the midst of suffering. Perhaps one of the most fundamental questions anyone ever asks is, *"Is hope more powerful than despair?"*

I know of a New York City inner-city mission that is trying to bring a message of hope to young people who receive very little hope. In this mission the counselors work with young people, many of them gang members or the victims of gang violence. Gangs are really a distorted cry for hope and community. The counselors wanted these youth to discover hope in everyday life, so they taught them about *mandalas*. A mandala is a circular piece of art that is a symbol of God's encompassing divinity. It is a symbol of a whole universe. Beautiful mandalas have been created throughout the centuries and have been preserved in books and museums. Admiring someone else's mandala, however, is not good enough. These counselors wanted the young people at their mission to discover hope for themselves.

They sent these kids out into the streets with large sheets of white paper and crayons and chalk and markers. The youth were to find different manhole covers and do rubbings of those covers. In so doing, they saw the intricacy of design, the beauty of the circles, symbols imbedded in the city streets. These symbols became signs of hope, of grace, and, yes, of God in the concrete city. Grace is the discovery that all of life is a gift and that the giftedness of this world is connected to God.

Victoria Ingram Curley was like most brides-to-be. She was picking out her beautiful white wedding dress. Getting the invitations out to friends. Making plans for the reception and honeymoon. A few months before her wedding, however, she learned that her fiancé was ill. Very ill. He would die unless he had a kidney transplant. Donors were sought, but none was suitable. Finally Victoria Ingram said: "What about me? Could I give him one of my kidneys?" Tests were made, and, remarkably, she was the perfect donor. The wedding was postponed, and a surgery was scheduled instead. When asked by the press why she would go through all of this, her answer was perfect: "This is what love is. This is what relationships are all about." She and her husband know something about grace!

The idea expressed by Paul of "being saved by grace" needs to be transformed to mean that we are made whole, that the pieces of our lives are glued back together. This happens in our lives when we realize that all of life is a gift and God's love for us never ceases. No wonder the message of the Christian faith was nicknamed *good news*!

OK. The pieces of our lives fly in different directions like a lightbulb dropped on the kitchen floor. That's our brokenness. The pieces are picked up and glued back together by the power of love and grace. That's our salvation. We can only trust grace. Receive it. Rely on it. That's our faith.

But then there is the ongoing experience of living a life. The life we live is pulled in two directions. On the one hand, we want to believe (trust and depend) on God's grace. On the other hand, we still get cancer and have loved ones killed in car wrecks and lose jobs and fail examinations and get divorces. Living hopefully does not mean bad things do not happen; it means that we face with courage the suffering that is presented to us and discover a hopeful power that comes to us through the presence of the Holy Spirit. Our reflection text is found right in the middle of Paul's third portrait in Romans, a portrait we might title "Keeping the Pieces Together."

In this text Paul writes about being "led by the Spirit." People who are led by the Spirit are, first of all, people who have acknowledged their own brokenness and fragmentation. This is not a weakness. It is a strength to recognize that you need God in your life. People led by the Spirit also have experienced the presence of God as a presence of grace and hope. God is love. And the Spirit is that ongoing presence of God—God's intimate, indwelling presence that provides the energy we need to live life fully and graciously.

Specifically, the Spirit does three things:

1. The Spirit leads us. For some, this idea of being led by the Spirit seems strange. How does the Spirit lead me? Does the Spirit literally whisper in my ear what job I should take, which person I should marry, what words I need to say in a difficult situation? Is this the leading of the Spirit? I must admit that I find myself a little uncomfortable around people who speak glibly of the Holy Spirit: "Well, God told me to do this or to say that." It's as if the Spirit is wired straight to their ear through some divine walkie-talkie system.

How do we know when *God* wants us to do something? How do we know it is the Spirit leading us and not just ourselves rationalizing that this is what God wants me to do when in fact it is what *I* want me to do?

A word that summarizes the leading of Spirit is the word *insight.* Anytime I have a new insight, I understand it as an expression of the Spirit's leading me and influencing me. Sometimes it is a new insight into myself. Sometimes it is a new insight into a relationship. A situation at work is sticky until a new insight happens. A church committee is bogged down until an insight begins to flow. The Spirit leads us by giving insight. Sometimes these insights are called "epiphanies." An epiphany is a moment of illumination, a time of seeing clearly, maybe only briefly, but clearly and deeply. One of Paul's most beautiful prayers can be found in the first chapter of Philippians when he prays that Christians will learn to let their love "overflow more and more with knowledge and full insight."

As I write this book, I'm on vacation with my family. I find that when I'm home I tend to be quiet, even withdrawn. I expend a lot of public energy as a minister, and when I get home, I just want to be left alone. Private. Quiet. On this trip, however, I am realizing that my family wants some of the same expressive energy that I give to the church week after week. In fact, they often experience my private quietness as abandonment and judgment toward them. That's not my intention, but that's what they feel.

This is a new insight for me. Although it is not one that is particularly easy for me to swallow, I know it is true. I take this insight as a sign that the Holy Spirit is leading my life. I want to learn to be more expressive at home. I want to learn to balance my public and private energy reservoirs. I want to give the best of my energy to the people I love the best, namely, my family. I want to follow this prompting of the Holy Spirit.

What's so wonderful about insights is that they are neither good nor bad. Insights are just insights. What we do with them is our choice, but they are there because the Spirit is offering them to us again and again. I find that the more I am conscious of the Spirit through Bible reading, prayer, and worship, the more insights I begin to have. When I am really walking with the Spirit, I see life in new and exciting ways. When I get caught up in schedules and stress, life becomes flat and deadly. Being led by the Spirit means being open to the insights of the Spirit.

It is helpful not to act on insights impulsively. It is helpful not to be obsessive about insights. It is helpful to have friends to talk to and say, "You know, I keep having this feeling, this intuition, this insight. What do you think?" Many of us have been programmed not to trust this inner feeling of the Spirit. We choose the guarded, rational, well-reasoned side of life. All of that is needed, but there is a part of the Spirit's leading that flows through the inner places of our soul, just a step beyond easy rational explanation.

2. The Spirit also prays for us. I absolutely love this idea. We can pray to God at any time, but there are moments—moments when suffering is so real, so deep, so devastating—that we cannot pray, that we do not know what to pray for or even how to pray. In those moments the Spirit is praying for us. Did you notice that the reflection text says *the Spirit intercedes with sighs too deep for words?* I used to think the Spirit had some special kind of prayer language that was beyond rational human language. I now understand that it is the Spirit who is praying for us while *we are groaning and aching and hurting.* When all we can do is cry, the Spirit prays on our behalf. When all we can do is sit in a chair trying to find enough energy just to get up and make a cup of coffee, the Spirit prays for us. It is true that the Spirit leads us by simply being with us.

In the Gospel of John the one word used most to describe the work of the Spirit is *Comforter.* (You can see this in such passages as John 14:17–18; John 16:13; and many others.) The Spirit's comforting work is not merely the soothing of feelings. Instead, it joins the strength of the Spirit with our strength. It fortifies us. It prepares us to go out and live life fully in the name of God. That's the comforting work of the Spirit.

One of the most moving books I have ever read was written by William Styron and titled *Darkness Visible: A Memoir of Madness.* It is the story of Styron's own battle with depression. Some of you, no doubt, know some of the private agony that goes along with depression. I have had times in my life when I felt overcome with a mysterious sadness or a dark kind of melancholy, though not depression, close enough that I can relate to this difficult state of being. Depression is the silent killer of many people. Styron wrote this book as a way of offering hope to others who deal with depression. His message is simple: *There is hope.* Depression does not need to be the whole story. Get help. Don't give up.

What touched me about his personal sharing was his deep appreciation for the friends who never gave up on him, especially when he was in his darkest time. When he was hospitalized certain friends wrote him weekly or called him daily. They were genuine companions in his suffering. That's exactly what the Holy Spirit is for us. When we seek to hold the pieces of our lives together, it is the Spirit that endures with us, prays for us, and never gives up on who are and who we can still become.

3. *The Spirit is an anticipatory sign of blessing.* The image Paul uses here is a little unusual, but it certainly makes the point clearly. When we are trying to hang on to our lives in the midst of suffering we wonder if there is any future.

What does the future hold? That question sometimes becomes an obsessively human one. The television stations are loaded with so-called "psychic hotlines" we can call and supposedly discover the future. We want to know the future. But when we are suffering, we wonder if there is a future at all.

Paul helped the Christians at Rome understand that even though life is hard right now, the future is bright because God has even more blessings to give. Which, of course, is a way of saying that God will continue loving people forever. Yes, forever! And the way Paul makes the point is by referring to the Holy Spirit as a *down payment.*

Most of us who have purchased a house know something about down payments. We take out a loan but give the bank a down payment as a sign that we will make good on the rest of the loan payments. You don't want to lose the investment of your down payment, so you do everything in your power to stay current with your loan payments. The Holy Spirit is God's down payment to you. There's more coming. There's more where that came from. God doesn't want to lose the initial investment in you. God is going to keep taking care of you, loving you, bringing wholeness to your life. The gift of God's Spirit is not the end but the beginning!

Flying to Atlanta recently, I sat beside a woman and her four children. She lived at the military base in Fort Knox but was headed to Atlanta and then Puerto Rico. She herself was Puerto Rican and started to tell me how she had not been home in ten years. Ten years is a long time. She was looking forward to seeing her mother, seeing old friends, being in the land of her childhood. Her mother had not even seen three of this woman's four children. What was

so beautiful about sitting beside her was that this woman was glow-
ing with hope and anticipation. She squirmed with delight as the
plane soared toward the south. She had so much hope. This kind
of anticipatory squirming is the work of the Spirit. We have no
need to fear the future—even death. The Spirit is a down payment, a sign of what is to come.

To be led by the Spirit is to move into the future with confidence, courage, and delight. What is to be feared? The Spirit gives
us insight for our living. The Spirit is a companion with us in
suffering. The Spirit gives us hope for our future. To live fully,
richly, hopefully—that's what it means to be a Christian. And that
is enough.

QUESTIONS FOR REFLECTION AND DISCUSSION

1. Why is hope so important to life?
2. Have you ever had a period in life when you lost hope? What
   was going on, and how did it feel?
3. Can you recall a time when you found hope again? How did
   it happen?
4. Hope is contagious. How can we better give people the gift
   of hope?
5. The idea of the Spirit's praying for us is a powerful one. What
   does it mean to you to know that the Holy Spirit prays for
   you each and every day?

12
WHAT
SPIRITS
YOUR LIFE
FORWARD?

Now there are varieties of gifts, but the same Spirit; and there are varieties of services, but the same Lord; and there are varieties of activities, but it is the same God who activates all of them in everyone. To each is given the manifestation of the Spirit for the common good. To one is given through the Spirit the utterance of wisdom, and to another the utterance of knowledge according to the same Spirit, to another faith by the same Spirit, to another gifts of healing by the one Spirit, to another the working of miracles, to another prophecy, to another the discernment of spirits, to another various kinds of tongues, to another the interpretation of tongues. All these are activated by one and the same Spirit, who allots to each one individually just as the Spirit chooses.

For just as the body is one and has many members, and all the members of the body, though many, are one body, so it is with Christ. For in the one Spirit we were all baptized into one body—Jews or Greeks, slaves or free—and we were all made to drink of one Spirit.

1 Corinthians 12:4–13

Life should move forward. I don't mean rushing headlong with breakneck speed, always wishing you are somewhere else. I don't mean wishing your life away and not being present in the moment. But moving forward means that there is a driving sense of purpose about who you are and what you are contributing to the world and, most importantly, living with a sense that "this is what God wants me to do." Moving forward means living radically in the ever-becoming now!

It's really too bad that the expression "getting turned on" has come to mean the activation of sexual feelings. Sexual feelings are wonderful, but the idea of getting turned on is not just sexual. *When was the last time you got turned on?* Turned on by a sunset? Turned on by a run along the beach or a walk through the woods? When was the last time you got turned on by teaching your class or taking care of a patient on your hospital ward or trying a case in the courtroom? When was the last time you got turned on in a conversation with a friend, talking about something that really meant something to you, touched your soul, gave you energy? When was the last time you got turned on to learning a new skill or exploring a new idea?

Getting turned on means being engaged, like gears moving or an engine turning over after a long stay in the garage. Activated. Alive. Aware. In tune. Tuned up. Spirited. Energized. To be turned on is to be in touch with life passion. This is the work of God's Spirit—bringing us to life and spiriting us forward into the world. Henry David Thoreau wrote from his little shack on Walden Pond, "I want to suck the very marrow out of life." How's that for being turned on?

Most of us treat life like a lollipop, taking an occasional genteel lick, but afraid to take a big bite and access the potential of life God calls us to embrace. I saw someone in Chicago wearing a T-shirt that read in big pink neon letters—LIVE JUICY! Living juicy means that we're alive to the energies and passions of life. We were created by God to be spirited forward into life. It is our spiritual destiny and calling.

The idea of calling is essential to our sense that life is moving forward. I want to dismiss a common misunderstanding about calling. Calling is not something that happens only to professional ministers. One of the questions I'm often asked when people learn I'm a minister is, "When were you called to the ministry?" Or better yet, "How old were you when you were called to be a minister?" I'm afraid I disappoint folks who are expecting some great story about lightning bolts striking my soul, the heavens opening up with a grand vision, and rolls of thunder punctuating this call to give my life to God in the ministry. That just didn't happen for me.

When I was a child, I remember being fascinated with the church. Call often begins with what fascinates us. I saw the minister in his robe each Sunday and felt a kind of holy feeling around him, around the bread and wine he handled at the communion table. Even the lighting of the candles, the procession of choir members, the oratory of his sermon created a feeling of fascination for me. And then there were the ideas. The ideas of discovering the meaning of life, the meaning of the Bible, the meaning of God in the world. It was fascination. And then you mix into that feeling my interest in helping make people's lives better. It all came together into a singular call to ministry.

Was God involved in my call? I have no doubt about it. But the call was a partnership of my interests and God's promptings, my talents and God's possibilities. And I need to say very quickly that the call is not finished. I don't have this feeling that God is finished with my call, and I certainly think there is more of my life call to be answered. In fact, I don't think our life call is ever really finished. I feel as if God is still calling me to move forward into life, offering the gifts of my life to the world, as well as developing new ones. Having a call is having a focus that culminates to the point that we say, "This is what God wants me to do." That is different for me today in my midlife years than it was in my childhood years when I first became fascinated with professional ministry. Your calling also changes and grows and shifts throughout your lifetime.

How is God calling you? Have you ever felt this sense of call, this wonderfully disturbing feeling that this is what God wants you to do? It's not so much a question of *whether* God is calling you as it is *how* and *in what way* God is calling you. Every person who is trying to follow the Spirit is being called, and being called is living the life that meaningfully spirits you forward.

Fred Wills had just retired from the military. For years he had dreamed of being free to do whatever he wanted to do whenever he wanted to do it. That seems to be the dream of most people as they contemplate retirement. No more early wake-up calls. No more long staff meetings. He didn't plan so much what he wanted to do as he knew what he didn't want to do. His pension was good. The good life seemed to be right around the corner. He and his wife, Betty, bought a house in Florida. Why not? The weather would be nice, and he wouldn't have to put up with all those cold winters in his hometown of Indianapolis.

Retirement went well—for about the first three months. Fred soon found himself getting bored. Restless. You can play only so much golf, and he wasn't about to be part of the shuffleboard crowd! He started having this nagging feeling, "Is this all there is?" The problem with retirement was not insufficient funds in his bank account. Their new house was nice too. What Fred was missing was this mysterious, wonderful, elusive sense of *call.*

A call did come. Actually a phone call. An old friend from Indianapolis called and told Fred about a community center that needed an executive director. He said, "The pay won't be much and the kids are a little on the rough side, but with your organizational ability and your experience with people, I thought you might be up for a new challenge." Fred thought about it and talked it over with his wife. The next day he was back on the phone accepting a new job and opening up a new vista for his retirement. For the first time since he retired, Fred Wills felt alive. The difference? A call.

There are two awarenesses I would offer about call. First, the Spirit's call is for *you*—not professional ministers alone. The Spirit calls *you* to the ministry of making a difference in this world. In the Christian tradition this dimension of every Christian's having a call, a ministry that he or she must answer, is occasionally referred to as the "priesthood of all believers." This is not to take away from those who are professional clergy. Professional ministers do for a living what everyone should be doing, to some extent or another, in their everyday life.

One of my best friends is Brother David Steindl-Rast. Brother David is a Benedictine monk, someone who lives in a monastery and prays and works in that religious community daily. He is a mystic, a contemplative. I've come to appreciate, however, that Brother David has his calling—living as a monastic hermit—and I have my calling—the public ministry of a congregation in the middle of a bustling city. He does around the clock what I need to do to some each day—namely, pray and contemplate and contribute to the building of world community.

I feel the same when I look at my congregation on Sunday morning. I am not better than they are. I'm not even more spiritual or more religious or even closer to God than the folks who sit in the pews and listen to me Sunday after Sunday. I might have some theological education that they do not have, perhaps a few experiences they have not experienced, but essentially we are the same. What I do professionally each day—caring for people, studying, praying, investing in the ministry of God on earth—is exactly what they need to be doing too. God calls me. God calls you. And that means we have a partnership in our quest to help each other listen for our respective callings from God. Call is a process shot through and through with mystery.

The second awareness I have is that call is the activation of *who we are as authentic human beings*—talents, time, potentials, personalities—offered for the well-being of others. Call is not passive. Call is not withdrawal. Call is discovering and putting to use what we are and what we can become. This discovery of what we have to offer the world is the discovery of our *spiritual gifts*. What Fred Wills discovered was that he had gifts and desires that needed to be put to use. Sitting in the Florida sun and playing golf every day wasn't enough. He had a call. When we find our call, use our gifts, develop our potentials, our lives spirit forward, and we feel ourselves alive. When we don't use our gifts, we become walking dead, hollow and without purpose. Call is essential to living.

In his book *The Seven Habits of Highly Effective People*, Stephen Covey challenges people to do self-inventory in order to search out what their lives are really all about. One exercise he suggests may at first sound a little strange, but I have found it to be both helpful and powerful. He asks people to imagine their own funeral. I know, it's not one of the happiest of thoughts we could have. But to imagine your own funeral and imagine what you would want said in your eulogy can be an enlightening experience. A eulogy holds the essentials of our lives.

What would you want said in your eulogy? Would you want people to highlight how much money you made? How many promotions you had? How many cars you purchased? How nice your clothes were? What is at the heart of your life?

Or would you want them to talk about the quality of your relationships? Would you like your children to talk about the essential character you gave them because you spent time with them? Would you want people to highlight how you gave something back to your church or your community? Would you want them to highlight something of your life mission? Would you want them to mention that your faith played a central role in your life? Would there be a unique calling mentioned in your eulogy?

In our reflection text from 1 Corinthians, Paul assumes that every Christian has a calling and that every Christian has gifts to give to it. There are a variety of ways to live one's calling authentically; it would be a big mistake to think that you need to become like someone else. Being a Christian does not mean becoming like someone else; it means becoming more and more like you. Sam Keen talks about the goal of life as the process of "giving birth to yourself." I think some of us have the mistaken notion that an ideal Christian exists whom we can take out of a cardboard box and then imitate the rest of our lives. Well, there is no ideal Christian. The Spirit wants us to learn to be who it is we are supposed to be.

Paul reminds the Corinthian church that some have the calling and gift of *wisdom*. These are people who seemingly have an uncanny capacity to bring insight to the lives of others. Not advice givers, mind you, but people with genuine skills of listening, summarizing, and sharing insights. Some have the gift of *knowledge*. By knowledge Paul means the capacity to appreciate and share the message of the Christian faith. I know theologians who have this gift. They have knowledge, information, technologies of the Spirit that can be helpful. Others have the gift of *faith*. Nothing seems to defeat their outlook and courage. Others have the gift of *healing*. That is to say, they know how to bring others to greater wholeness, know how to put life pieces back together. Persons who are good listeners are healers. Persons who have the capacity to make others laugh are healers. Paul was not trying to give an exhaustive list of all the spiritual gifts that have ever existed as much as he was trying to give the church an idea of the many ways of authentically serving others. He was trying to bring to consciousness that every Christian needs to do spiritual inventory and offer gifts to the world.

I've been trying to imagine what Paul's list might look like today if he were encouraging persons in our culture to imagine their gifts. What gifts might be most needed now? I want to suggest three critical spiritual gifts we need to discover if we want our lives to spirit forward effectively in our world.

1. Discover the spiritual gift of appreciating diversity. To say that we live in a diverse world is to state the obvious. There is racial diversity. Ethnic diversity. Lifestyle diversity. Economic diversity. Educational diversity. When I was growing up, the world was much simpler. Dads did what dads did. Moms typically stayed home and did what moms did. Nobody asked any questions. The good guys wore the white hats, and the bad guys wore the black hats. Everything and everyone and every type of person knew his or her place. A clearly defined social order was at the center of American culture.

Since my childhood, however, the world has exploded in its awareness of diversity. The civil rights movement brought to my consciousness that there were other citizens in this country besides the middle-class white family from which I came. The feminist movement brought to my consciousness that women cannot be kept in their so-called place; they have talents and feelings and potentials to be offered to the world. My appreciation has grown for the role of the Native American peoples in the history of this country. My appreciation for the plight of children continues to be highlighted by advocacy groups. The needs of older adults are now being rethought and retaught as our understanding of aging has been enlarged. The Berlin Wall has come down, and those who were once enemies have now become diverse allies. Russians and Americans are now exploring space—not as madness-driven competitors, but as friends and partners. Diversity has now become part of the picture.

This powerful presence of diversity, however, sometimes over-whelms people, and they begin thinking that diversity really doesn't matter or, worse, they overreact and become entrenched, angrily guarding what they perceive as their piece of the social turf. Why is it, after all, that in spite of the growing diversity in our culture, we see a rise in hate crimes, a rise in militia movements, a rise in heated, if not hateful, diatribes over the airwaves? Why the backlash of resentment? You would think that white supremacy groups would be a thing of the past. But, tragically, they continue to exist. Why has the world become more dangerous and not less?

It seems to me that one way of thinking about diversity is not in some abstract way, such as how I should treat African Americans or how I should treat women or how I should treat any particular group, but in a personal way, making diversity more of a relationship matter. When this happens you can find yourself asking:

"How can I see God in the face of this person?"

"What is this person needing to teach me?"

"How can I grow as a person by being in the presence of this man or woman?"

One of the most fundamental questions our culture is asking—and which you as a Christian can help answer—is *"Do we need each other?"* Just because a person doesn't live in my neighborhood, my country, or my hemisphere doesn't mean I don't need him or her. I need the Jewish child living in Brooklyn. I need the Bosnian refugee. I need the woman in Los Angeles trying to break into a law firm for her first job. I need the rural Appalachian couple. I need the wealthy family of Beacon Hill in Boston. We need the fellow citizens of God's world.

I once heard the story of the man who one day was down and depressed in a small Italian village. He went to see a doctor and tried to explain, "I don't feel as if I have any energy. I don't have any real friends. I go around all day and feel blue. What do you think I should do?"

The doctor thought a minute and suddenly a lightbulb went on: "I've got a great idea. There's a man in town today who will perform a show. He makes people laugh. He entertains. He brings much happiness to people's heart. You should go see him. His name is the Great Grimaldi!"

The patient looked more downcast than ever. He hung his head and muttered, "I am the Great Grimaldi!"

Everybody needs somebody. Even the Great Grimaldi. Diversity should serve to make that point clearer and more urgent—we need each other.

One gift that is needed to move life forward for all people in our world today is the gift of appreciating diversity. If you as one person can learn effectively to build bridges between people, have conversations that bring folks together rather than split them apart, then you will have made a tremendous contribution to this world. If you can learn to speak the word of tolerance, acceptance, and love in conversations, then you begin moving life forward, not only for yourself, but for others who are counting on you to speak a word of appreciation for diversity. I like to think about it like this: there is always someone out there whose sense of worth is depending on how I speak about him or treat her. You may not win a Nobel Peace Prize. You don't have to. But what you can win is the approval of Jesus Christ who said, "Blessed are the peacemakers, for they shall be called the children of God."

2. Discover the gift of enhancing family life. I don't mean to be exclusive when I use the word "family," because many single people are active in the church and growing in their faith. I think a single person is a family. At the same time, it's important to recognize that families need help; they need strength; and they need to discover the focus of the Spirit in order to live more effectively.

Families are in tough times. The pressures on my teenagers are not what I had to face. I had to decide whom I would take to the prom; they face the issues of AIDS, unprecedented violence in their schools, rampant abuse of alcohol and drugs that is demoralizing many of our college campuses, a suicide rate among teens that has soared in the last twenty years, and a shrinking job market that is causing a sense of hopelessness among some of the young. I grew up under the threatening clouds of communism and the atomic bomb. The pressures on teenagers and children today are more internal and certainly more real.

In light of some of these issues, there is a call by some to get back to "old-fashioned values," back to the "good old days," back to the "traditional family values" that will make families strong again. "If we can just go back," some reason, "we can then go forward."

I appreciate these sentiments. I really do. Someone asked me the other day, "Do you know what a conservative is?" I said, "No, tell me." "A conservative is a liberal with a teenage daughter!" I know a little bit of this feeling of wanting to protect a teenage daughter—and two teenage sons. As a parent I sometimes get plain old-fashioned scared for my kids. I want them to grow up and be strong and healthy and enjoy life. And, most of all, I want them to learn to live in God.

However, what if the answer for families today is not going back to Ward and June Cleaver and the perfect *Leave It to Beaver* family? What if the answer is not turning back to the last page, but moving forward to the next page? What if what is urgently needed today is for Christian moms and Christian dads to forge a new way of loving and leading their families? That will require the spiritual gift of family nurture.

What might that gift of family nurture look like?

First of all, if the family is a two-parent family, then Mom and Dad need to envision their parenting work as a partnership. Not Mom in charge of the kids. Not Dad taking care of the yard and doing the barbecue. Partners. Both doing the essential nurturing and disciplining. Children, insofar as it is possible, need positive male and female leadership.

Second, families need to create clear boundaries and consequences of actions. Discipline is not just sporadic spanking or capricious grounding. Actions have consequences, and families need to teach that. Family is where ethics are first learned. Telling the truth does matter. Sharing does matter. Waiting my turn does matter. I've often thought that if children were taught basic manners most of their ethical decisions would be easy. Decisions and actions have consequences, and parents cannot exempt their children from this truth.

Third, families need to be the place where creativity and problem-solving skills are learned. Problems don't blow families apart, nor do problems drive families into closets to keep secrets. Families need to be the place where everyone can share his or her feelings and where solutions are discovered for the well-being of all people in the family. Listening skills and speaking skills are crucial.

Fourth, families need to be places of soulful life. Families have souls and these souls are nurtured by rituals such as praying for dinner or saying prayers at bedtime or going to church together. Families need to do things together, not to create some idealized situation they think they should fulfill, but to learn how to generate common energy. Stories need to be developed and told in families. It's not enough to do things for our families; our families need to touch their unique soul.

Fifth, families need to be places of learning. The schools will do their part, but the schools cannot do it all. It's not enough that children learn information. Will they learn the joy of reading, the wonder of art and music, the ecstasy of physical activity? Education is not completing high school or college; it is touching this feeling of aliveness that comes with using the gift of body and mind. This is the deepest human dimension. Not mindless watching of television. But thinking and feeling. These are the essentials of human spirit that are nurtured in families.

Consequently, although Paul did not mention it as a spiritual gift, there is little doubt in my mind that we need to practice the gift of nurturing family life. If done well, our families can become cathedrals of hope for our churches and world.

3. Discover the gift of building church. I add this as a crucial spiritual gift because I don't think it has ever been more difficult to be "church" in American culture than it is right now. In the 1950s people were flocking to American churches. All you needed was a strategically located building, usually on a prominent town corner, a good minister, and a good music program, and you had the ingredients for a successful church. It was a time when the economy was growing quickly, and families were growing too. During this time there also was a general cultural consensus that going to church was both a good thing and a right thing. Church membership was part of a larger cultural package of being a good, solid middle-class citizen.

During the 1960s this larger cultural picture began cracking like a frozen lake on the first day of spring. Institutions became not friends, but enemies during the 1960s. Vietnam was devastating. In light of recent remarks by Robert McNamara regarding the lies about the war, those old institutional suspicions seem only reinforced. Part of the reason why movies such as *Forrest Gump* touch such a deep cultural nerve is that, for many of us, our whole understanding of institutional life changed in the 1960s. A president and vice-president resigned in shame, serving only to weaken institutional appreciation. Corporations plundered natural resources without thought to environmental concerns. It was a tough time for institutions.

This noninstitutional mindset continues today as baby boomers and now the boomlets called Generation X make their way to church. If they come to church at all, it is certainly not because it is a good or accepted thing to do culturally speaking. They come to church now because they are interested in finding some spiritual answer for their lives, some meaning for their existence, and perhaps some stability and spiritual grounding for the lives of their children. These are good reasons to come to church, and I applaud any person or family who comes to church these days.

The difference, however, in comparison to a 1950s family, is that people today primarily see the church as a place to get their needs met and not as a place where they are called to worship regularly, work on committees, serve on church boards, and give sacrificially of their money in order to build the church. But that transition has to be bridged. Building church is a gift that has to be rediscovered!

There are some, obviously, who are spiriting forward into life and using this gift. But their stories need to become more and more widespread. I know a young family who gives 10 percent of their income and investments to the church every year. That's church building. I know a stockbroker who takes a week of his vacation each year to go with a youth group on a musical tour. That's church building. I know a couple who prayed long and hard when he was asked to assume the chairmanship of the church board. She said she would do all she could to keep things going at home so that he would have time to do this ministry. That's building church.

And what I know from my own experience is that some of the loneliest people in the world are ministers—probably your minister. They many times feel as if they are the only ones who really care, who are really committed, who really want to build the church. Sometimes that can lapse into whining or needless self-righteousness, but there is also a sense that your minister would love to know that you are really with him or her, that you are willing to sacrifice to make the church all it can be, that you will walk through hell with your minister because ultimately the church is worth it!

The church has to move:

From a place to get, to a place to give;

From a place to harvest, to a place to sow;

From a place where I am served, to a place where I serve;

From a place that belongs to the pastor, to a place that belongs to the people;

From a place where I attend, to a place where I participate.

Gary is a young man in my congregation. I love his enthusiasm. He has a buoyant kind of energy I find contagious. He came up to me after a sermon a few weeks ago and said, "You need some of us young bucks to get this place moving again. Use us. We're ready!" Wow! You cannot imagine the power of his words to my soul. And I guarantee that your pastor is just waiting to hear words like that; he or she is ready to lock arms with you and build the community.

The Spirit has many gifts, and what's even more remarkable is that you have some of them! What exactly they are is your adventure to live, but I know you have them. God is calling you. God has some mission for your life. To experience the Spirit sometimes calls us to throw ourselves into the arena of life that is lived for others. Maybe our gifts will move toward the city or the family or the church. (Why not all three?) To find the Spirit is finally done only when we, in the words of Jesus, "lose ourselves." The Spirit gives you and me a gift—it is the gift of reinventing our lives. That's the remarkable possibility of faith. What we have been is nothing compared to what we can become. Spiriting forward is what it's all about. Don't settle for the past. Don't live in a rut. Don't do what you've always done. The creative, transforming work of God is alive inside of you.

I heard Joel Barker tell of a time when he saw what looked like a man dancing in the spray of ocean waves. At least it appeared that he was dancing. From a distance it looked as if the man swooped way low, then turned dramatically, and finally flung his body into the ocean. Barker was so curious that he walked closer to the man. As he got closer he could see that the man was not dancing at all. Instead, he was bending down, picking up starfish that the surf had thrown upon the shore, and tossing them back into the ocean.

Barker asked him, "Why are you doing this?"

The man responded, "I come out here every morning and try to throw all of the starfish back into the ocean before the morning sun burns them up."

"But don't you know," Barker asked, "that there are hundreds of miles of coast and millions of starfish? Do you really think you're making a difference?"

The man paused for a moment, then bent down to pick up a starfish. Holding it in his hands he said, "It makes a difference to this one." And with that one comment, he whirled around and threw the starfish into the ocean.

Who you are—your gifts, your passions, your skills—does make a difference. The Spirit leads you forward to the world, and the church; the Spirit moves you to give the best of your gifts to others. Who you are is your unique dance, your way of putting something back into the great world of God.

QUESTIONS FOR REFLECTION AND DISCUSSION

1. Right now, would you describe your place in life as going backward, forward, or staying about the same?
2. Have you ever had this feeling of calling, this feeling of God's wanting you to do something? What is it? How would you describe it?
3. What are your spiritual gifts?
4. When have you used your spiritual gifts for the well-being of others? What did it feel like afterward?
5. As you look at the world and church today, what gifts do you think we need now more than ever?

SUGGESTED READING

Often I'm asked what people can read to enhance their faith. This is difficult to answer for several reasons. First, there are a lot of books out there! I mean a *lot* of books. If you go to your local Christian bookstore, you'll probably be confused by the number of different kinds of books. Second, there are several good books out there, but many of them are written for a university or seminary context. These are normally, but not always, too difficult for the Christian who wants a casual introduction to the faith. Additionally, there are different books representing different perspectives on the faith. Some may be too conservative. Others may seem too liberal. This is why recommending books is difficult.

What I have tried to do in this book is to reach people who are taking their first theological steps. Nothing profound. Nothing too complicated. Just opening the door to the process of understanding and deepening faith. I know there are other books that are helpful, and I want to suggest some to you. These aren't necessarily the best or even the latest books on the market. This list represents some books I would feel comfortable recommending to people in my own congregation. There's nothing better than a good book. I would encourage you to turn off the television and read!

1. *Building a Biblical Faith* by Charles Bayer. This is one of the best and most recent works for theological insight written for people in churches. The book is simple, but never simplistic. I

think it would make for a great study book in a church school class.

2. *Where in the World Is God?* by Robert Brizee. This book effectively addresses the issue of how God works in the world. This is one of the most important theological matters about which we can ever think. This book is easy to understand and offers an alternative to the various Christian ideas that exist regarding the presence of God in the world.

3. *Creation Spirituality*, by Matthew Fox. This is a simple introduction to the thinking of Matthew Fox. In recent years, Fox has developed a religious movement called "Creation Spirituality." His ideas are excellent. His approach to the faith is holistic and honors the whole creation. I find his writing exciting and accessible.

4. *Mere Christianity*, by C. S. Lewis. This book deeply influenced me when I was in college. It's really not all that easy a book to read, but in recent years it has become a classic. The theology of the book is traditional, more traditional than what I'm used to; nevertheless, I like the book. It's readily available, and the story of C. S. Lewis is interesting. I think you might like it if you want a good intellectual challenge.

5. *New Seeds of Contemplation*, by Thomas Merton. I love all the writings of Thomas Merton. His understanding of prayer continues to shape who I am. I have visited his monastery in Kentucky and often have felt close to his spirit, even though he has been dead for nearly twenty years. Merton brought the Christian faith into conversation with literature, poetry, science, social issues, and Eastern thinking. This particular book is excellent and easy to read. Don't let the simplicity of the essays fool you; every one of them is profound and deserves careful contemplation.

6. *The Meaning of Revelation*, by H. Richard Niebuhr. This is a little book, but one upon which I have drawn time and time again. Niebuhr was one of America's greatest theologians. In this simple book, he captured brilliantly some of the most profound truths of the Christian faith. I should warn you that he addresses certain philosophical concerns that were going on when he wrote, which makes this book at times read more like a college textbook than a layperson's volume. Yet, if you've had any philosophy in

college or any introductory course in religion, you will enjoy this book.

7. *The Active Life*, by Parker Palmer. I like this book and the approach it offers to spirituality. Palmer tells stories and speaks from the heart. He offers a view of the spiritual life that is something other than monastic. I can see a study group really enjoying this book. I also like Palmer's balanced approach to the faith. Nothing too much to the right or left. It is solid, and I think you would like it.

8. *Honest to God*, by John A. T. Robinson. I'm sorry to tell you that this is an old book, but I'm happy to tell you that it is the best introduction to modern theological thinking of which I know. You might think it a little heavy, but hang in there. Some streams are worth wading. It's probably written on a college level. When this book came out in the 1960s, it rocked the theological world! It's still worth reading.

9. *A Pretty Good Person*, by Lewis Smedes. This is about the most accessible book on daily Christian ethical living that I've ever read. It's responsible and fun to read. And I would suggest it for a group or an individual. I discovered it a few years ago and have used it in my preaching over and over again. What I like best about this book is that it is real. No jargon. No heavy-handed theological ideas. Smedes writes where people live. I hope you enjoy it.

10. *Gratefulness, the Heart of Prayer*, by David Steindl-Rast. In the last ten years no one has touched my faith more than Brother David. He's a Benedictine monk, who offers his gifts of teaching and writing to the world. I love this book. It is beautiful. Poetic. And theologically it is exactly where I live. If you can get only one book on this list, then get this one. Brother David uses simple images to break open profound ideas. Don't read this book quickly. Let it become a life companion. Brother David has been called the "Thomas Merton for our generation." I think it's better to say he has become the "Brother David for our generation."